Reflections

To Joan,

I was blessed

with you in my class

Mike

Reflections

A Collection of Stories
From the Past

Compiled and edited by Susan L. Shisler

ISBN-13: 978-1512197693
ISBN-10: 1512197696

Library of Congress Control Number: 2015908989

Susan L. Shisler
East Amherst, NY

susan.shisler@ymail.com

Printed by CreateSpace, Charleston SC
An Amazon.com Company

This book is dedicated to the wonderful and inspiring members of the Clarence Senior Center and to senior adults everywhere. Your stories from the past create history for the future.

Table of Contents

Preface

From the time we're youngsters, stories often play an important role in our lives, teaching valuable lessons, sparking imaginations, and creating lasting memories. Family history and traditions, as well as personal life experiences, are passed down from generation to generation through stories told by parents and grandparents. While nothing is better than hearing those stories first hand, putting them in writing is the best way to make sure they're remembered for generations to come.

Several years ago I read *When I Was Your Age* by Bill Westley, a member of the Clarence Senior Center where I formerly worked as the office manager. For years Bill had included notes in the birthday cards of his grandchildren telling them what his life had been like at whatever age they were turning. Eventually he put all the notes together and created a book that tells his life story. What a treasure for his family! I've always enjoyed reading biographies, and Bill's was no exception.

One day while chatting with my good friend Karla Madrid, the executive director of the Clarence Senior Center, she told me a couple stories that had been shared at the annual nonagenarian luncheon—a birthday celebration for members in their nineties. After I remarked that the stories would make a great book, Karla, in a not too subtle "hint hint," asked if I knew anyone who liked to write. She gave me the inspiration I needed, and I only had to think about it for a day or two before the idea for this book flourished.

When the first story I received was from Bob Poczik, a well-respected member of the Center who often gives entertaining presentations, I knew the book was off to a good start. I then received a story from Marge McMillen, who has written six books of her own, another good sign. As word got around, I gradually received the twenty-two stories included in *Reflections*. The stories represent many diverse backgrounds and portray a wide range of events, experiences, and emotions. Half of the stories were self-written and half were a joint effort between the individuals and me.

Creating this anthology has been an incredibly gratifying experience. In addition to becoming better acquainted with each of the storytellers, which I thoroughly enjoyed, I gained a wealth of information about a wide variety of topics. From Fort Niagara and the now defunct Civic Stadium to LCIs and F-5s, from Germany, France and the Philippines to Norway and India, and from the Roosevelts and English bulldogs to Visniak pop and apple cider, I researched each story to verify facts and understand circumstances. I learned what it was like to be a child in the midst of war, a sailor going off to war, and a soldier coming home. As I immersed myself in the stories, I could visualize the merriment of family events and the thrill of things accomplished. I could feel the deep emotion as folks talked about their mothers, their children, their pets, and their careers. But most importantly I learned about the resilience, the hard work, the creativity, and the enthusiasm of the twenty-two storytellers you are about to meet.

I hope you enjoy these nostalgic reflections as much as I have. I would love to hear your feedback, and I would love to hear YOUR story. Contact me at susan.shisler@ymail.com or PO Box 484, East Amherst, NY 14051.

~ *Susan*

Acknowledgments

My heartfelt appreciation, first of all, to the individuals who so willingly shared their stories for this book...it would not have been possible without you!

I am also grateful to:

The many others who offered encouragement and helped spread the word about this project, especially Violet Oldenski and Marge McMillen; Karla Madrid and the rest of the staff at the Clarence Senior Center for all their support in bringing *Reflections* to fruition; and Edna Scherf, who graciously offered some last minute editing assistance.

Lastly, many thanks to my husband, Pete, and children, Tim and Jessica (and fiancé John), for their constant love, support, ideas, and feedback. Thank you, thank you, thank you!

The Kiss

Mary Morris

When I was a young girl, nearly ten years old, I witnessed something I will always remember. The scene was Seymour Street in East Buffalo, NY in August of 1934. The New York Central train tracks ran behind the homes on Seymour, and train traffic headed to and from the Buffalo Central Terminal was a common sight.

It was a hot summer day when a neighbor loudly knocked on our side door, calling to my mother, "Alice! Alice! The train is stuck on the tracks and our President is on the train!" My mama, as I fondly called her, grabbed my arm and literally pulled my frail body with her as she ran out the door and headed toward the tracks. Down the street, over rocks, through a ditch, and up a hill we ran, joining our neighbors to catch a glimpse of the President.

Once we reached the train, still motionless on the tracks, we could see one open window, and there was President

Franklin D. Roosevelt sitting in his wheelchair waving and blowing kisses to the small crowd that had gathered alongside the train. As we drew near, the President motioned to Mama to come closer and told her to lift me up to him, which she did. He asked my name, then placed his hands on my face and kissed my forehead as all the neighbors clapped! After Mama set me down the President loudly declared, "Mary, when you grow old like some of the people here, you won't have to worry about paying your bills. As soon as I get home I am having a meeting with Congress about this plan of mine. And in the future don't let anyone in Washington try to change my plan, because it won't work!"

As the train finally began to make its way along the tracks, the neighbors all went home in wonder. About a year later, on August 14, 1935, President Roosevelt signed the Social Security Act. Recalling the words the President had proclaimed from the train, neighbors on Seymour Street danced with joy, shouting "God bless our President!" And I grew up to tell my story, "I was kissed by the President!"

Hello World

June Grier

I grew up on Gerhardt Street in Buffalo, a block from Civic Stadium and ten minutes from downtown. I was the oldest child of five, with two younger brothers and two younger sisters. Having been born on the heels of the depression and a mere child through the war years, my formative days coincided with a time of growth and stability for the city. In 1957 my sisters and I had the opportunity to be part of an exciting and historical event.

As I said, Civic Stadium, later renamed War Memorial Stadium, was a stone's throw from our house. It loomed large in the neighborhood, and our lives were very tied to the enormous, bowl-shaped structure. Before it became the first home to the Buffalo Bills, the stadium was used for parades, circuses, ball games, and mini-car races. The days and evenings on which these events were held always brought excitement to the close-knit neighborhood. All the neighbors would offer our front yards and driveways as parking for folks attending these events, charging $5 to park on the lawn and $2 for a spot in the driveway. Then we'd keep an eye on the cars until the event was over and all the cars were safely driven away by their owners. It was always great fun and we eagerly looked forward to each event.

With five kids my father worked hard to provide a living for all of us. In addition to working as a butcher, he became a vendor at the stadium selling beer and peanuts at the races and ball games to bring in some extra money. There were several entrances into the stadium. The one on Dodge Street, commonly referred to as "The Pit," was used to bring the unusual looking mini-cars in for the races. It was also the entrance that athletes used to come into the stadium. We often hung out by The Pit, so most everyone who worked there knew us as "the vendor's kids." When I was about twelve years old my brothers and I, lured by the sound of the mini-cars racing around the stadium, attempted to pull out a section of fence to sneak in. But an observant security guard saw us and, after an obligatory scolding, reminded us that our father worked there and that we could come into the stadium through the entrance whenever we wanted to!

So in 1957 when I was asked by Dorothy, the woman I taught Sunday school with, to participate in Buffalo's 125th Anniversary Celebration at Civic Stadium, it didn't take too much cajoling. Actually the week-long event, to be called the "World Port Celebration," would feature activities throughout the city. But Dorothy, insisting that my sisters and I "would be adorable," was recruiting volunteers for "Hello World," a reenactment of the history of Buffalo. I was nineteen years old then and working at M&T Bank, and in addition to volunteering at Concordia Lutheran Church, I also volunteered as a Girl Scout leader. I was a busy young woman, but after conferring with my sisters, Marie and Dorothy, who were thirteen and fifteen respectively, we eagerly accepted the invitation to participate in the celebration.

The spectacular event with thousands of volunteers was scheduled for September 20-29. About a week before the first show, all the participants in the segment of "Hello World" that my sisters and I would be part of gathered at the Lutheran church for a brief rehearsal and to pick up our costumes. About fifty or sixty of us, young and old, would "greet the train carrying Abraham Lincoln," reenacting when the President-elect stopped in Buffalo on his way to Washington for his inauguration in 1861. My sisters and I were given long flowered dresses to wear (which I believe were provided by the Historical Society) along with flat, saucer-like hats that we pinned to our heads. Our excitement grew; we'd seen many events held at Civic Stadium, but this was the biggest and we were going to be a part of it!

(L to R) Me, Dorothy, and Marie dressed for "Hello World"

Opening night was a Friday. "Hello World" was to start at 8:30 in the evening, somewhat late for my sisters who were still in school. In spite of my excitement, my thoughts as we took the short walk to the stadium were focused more on keeping track of Marie and Dorothy in the great crowds of people. We gathered with our group outside The Pit, which of course we were so familiar with, and waited for our cue to enter the stadium. Amazingly, actual train tracks had been installed for the festivities, and two train cars—an engine and a caboose—would take the short ride into the stadium carrying a well-portrayed Abraham Lincoln.

At the time, Civic Stadium had about 35,000 seats, and on the evening of September 20, 1957 there was a full crowd in attendance. When our moment finally arrived and the train slowly headed into the stadium, the entourage, all dressed in 1860s attire, followed behind clapping and cheering loudly. The train came to a stop in the middle of the stadium and the President-elect, with his long beard and tall hat, stepped out to address the crowd. We cheered and clapped at the designated times as Lincoln's reenactor proclaimed his words from 1861. After the speech had been delivered and our applause subsided, the train circled back to the entrance as the lights dimmed so we could make our exit and the stage could be set for the next reenactment. My sisters and I walked home as soon as our segment was done, then donned our long flowered dresses to repeat the performance each evening throughout the week.

I never did see any other parts of "Hello World," but it was an exciting time for the neighborhood and the whole city of Buffalo. I have many fond memories of the events at Civic Stadium over the years, and participating in Buffalo's 125th Anniversary Celebration was definitely one of the most thrilling and memorable.

Meeting Eleanor

Bob Poczik

In 1961 I was a sophomore at Harpur College, which later became the State University at Binghamton but was then a very new, small liberal arts college. About twenty sophomore students formed an International Relations Club at the college, and I was elected Vice-President. At one of our meetings we decided to invite Eleanor Roosevelt to come to the college to make a speech in honor of United Nations Day, which is celebrated on October 24 each year, and I was delegated to write the letter of invitation.

A few weeks later we received a response from Mrs. Roosevelt's personal secretary letting us know that Mrs. Roosevelt could only come if an honorarium and her airfare were paid. Since the club had no treasury, I wrote back saying that we were very sorry but we could not provide what was required. We were then surprised to receive a second letter from her secretary informing us that Mrs. Roosevelt had decided she would come to the college anyway.

Now, we had neglected to let the college administration know that we had extended this invitation, so it caused quite a stir when we made a request for the college auditorium for Mrs. Roosevelt's speech. To put this in some perspective, in 1961, Eleanor Roosevelt had been voted the Most Admired Woman in America for the twelfth consecutive year. She was known and admired worldwide. So her coming to the college was a bigger deal than we had anticipated, and the college hastily made plans for her proper reception.

The college arranged for a limousine to bring Mrs. Roosevelt from the Binghamton airport, and the officers of the club, me included, were taken in the limo to greet her and escort her to the college. So with a police escort, we went to the airport, where Mrs. Roosevelt arrived on a small, propeller-driven plane operated by Mohawk Airlines. She came slowly down the steps from the plane and walked to the terminal building. We escorted her through a throng of applauding people with flashing cameras and spoke excitedly to her all the way through the terminal and into the limo.

Once inside the limousine, Mrs. Roosevelt reached inside her coat and switched on her hearing aid! She explained that she always turned it off in crowded situations and just smiled and waved to everyone. Our conversation with her in the limo was amazing. I had read quite a lot about Franklin Roosevelt and the New Deal, and it was remarkable to hear her say things like, "Now Harry (meaning Harry Hopkins) always used to say to Franklin..." She was talking about people she had known personally but who were figures in history to us as students. She herself was living history.

Her speech at the college was a huge success and was delivered to a packed auditorium, with an additional crowd of people standing outside in the lobby and watching her on TV. It was very special for me when she signed a copy of her autobiography I had purchased as a gift for my mother: "With warm good wishes, Eleanor Roosevelt." My mother treasured the book, and now that she has passed away, it is one of my treasures.

Recently, as I reflected on this event, I wondered how old Eleanor Roosevelt had been in 1961. It turned out that she was seventy-seven, and she passed away at age seventy-eight in November of 1962, the following year. How remarkable it was that in the last year of her life, when she was undoubtedly ill, she got on a tiny propeller-driven airplane and flew from New York City to Binghamton because a small group of college students without any funds thought that it was important and fitting to pay honor to her beloved United Nations.

College Days

The Tornado

Fred Kintzel

In 1989 I experienced something that has remained vividly in my memory ever since. I was working as a New York State corrections officer and had been assigned to the Green Haven Correctional Facility near the New York/Connecticut border. We were living in South Buffalo, too far for a daily commute, so I stayed in the housing provided for employees during my work week and drove home for my days off.

On Thursday, November 16, 1989 I left home early in the morning for the six hour trip back to work. As I approached the little town of Newburgh, about fifty miles north of New York City and forty-five minutes from Green Haven, the sky started to get dark and the wind and rain became stronger. I didn't need to get gas in my car, but for some reason that I can't explain, I decided that I would get some anyway at the next gas station. At approximately 12:30 p.m. I drove by an elementary school and pulled into a gas station that was a few hundred yards past the school.

As I got out of my car and started pumping gas, the sky suddenly turned extremely dark and the wind and rain became alarmingly strong. I quickly ducked behind the pump for protection. I had never before seen such fierce wind—it was literally driving the rain horizontally. As I crouched behind the pump, I could see the clerk inside the store watching me through the window.

It seemed to subside as quickly as it had started, and then there was an eerie quiet. After paying for the gas I had pumped, which was $1.63 (it's funny how I remember that small amount) I got back in my car and started back to work. Looking both ways before entering the highway, I immediately knew something bad had happened. There was a tree lying across the road in the direction I had come from, and debris was littered everywhere. I started hearing sirens blaring from all directions as I cautiously made my way down the road. Within a few minutes, both the sky and the road in front of me were clear.

I continued on to work and was very happy to arrive safely. As the day went on I began seeing and hearing news reports of a possible tornado or hurricane that had hit the Newburgh area. And then there was news that an elementary school had been hit. Reports said that a large glass wall in the school cafeteria had blown in as children were eating their lunches. Seven children, all seven and eight years old, were killed, and many more were seriously injured. I thought of the school I had passed just before stopping for gas, but I didn't know if that was the school that had been hit.

It wasn't until I was returning home several days later that I found out that it was, in fact, the same elementary school. As I drove past the school I saw that the windows were boarded up and hundreds of flowers and crosses had been placed in front of the school. A chill went through me as I thought of the children. I found out later that two more had died of their injuries in the days that followed.

For the next four months that I worked at the Green Haven Correctional Facility and passed the school on my weekly drive, I always remembered those children with a prayer. I will never forget how close I was to that tragedy as it unfolded and have often wondered why I stopped for gas when I really didn't need to.

Graduation in 1989

The Bungalow

Bill Westley

Most folks call them cottages or cabins, but our summer place was always called "the bungalow," and several generations of Westleys spent many a happy summer there. My dad bought the bungalow on the Maiden Creek in Reading, Pennsylvania in 1927 when he was twenty-six years old and single. It was about a half mile downstream from the Reading water supply, called Lake Ontelaunee, and the water was good and clean. The bungalow, which sat on piers and had no basement, trees, or neighbors when Dad bought it, somehow earned the formal name of "Sunny Nest." I never did learn how the name came to be, and, regardless, we always just called it "the bungalow."

In the early years my dad and his friends dug a basement by hand and moved the dirt and stone to the eroded creek edge. The basement walls were constructed, the floor cemented, and the porch was added. I always knew the work was done before 1932 because my baby footprints were on one of the columns. Originally the basement was a garage, a guest changing area, and a storage space, but that function would change many times during the sixty-four years of Westley ownership. There was no electricity or plumbing in those early years. We had a white gas stove, kerosene lamps, and an icebox, and we carried water in buckets from the spring about a block away. Our toilet was an outhouse, and we washed in the creek. There was a rain water barrel that collected soft water for dishwashing and for the women to wash their hair. Trees were transplanted from Lake Ontelaunee and planted around the bungalow, and many of our meals were on the picnic table by the creek and fireplace.

The bungalow in 1928

A volleyball game at the bungalow in 1931

A few years after my dad bought his place, my grandparents, Grammom and Grampop Beane, built a bungalow next door. By that time there were a few other bungalows as well as forty or fifty decks with tents. We lived in luxury compared to the people in the tents. The earliest improvement I remember is enclosing the porch. My dad borrowed the company truck and bought some used window frames from a factory that was being demolished. He permanently mounted half of them and hung the other half on rollers to open or close as the weather dictated. It was just before World War II when we received electricity. My dad did all the wiring, and a neighbor, "Gus Long, Electrician," inspected and approved it. We replaced our appliances in the city with new ones and moved the old appliances to the bungalow.

After WWII a few of the neighbors went together and had a well dug. It was close to our bungalow and was operated with a hand pump. We still needed buckets, but at least the trip was shorter than before. I would be in my forties when Dad had a well dug next to the bungalow and plumbed the place for running water. We still used the outhouse, though, because there was no good place for a leach field.

In the summer of 1940 my mom was pregnant and decided to have the baby at the bungalow. It was a hot Saturday night on July 20, 1940 when my mom went into labor. I was sent next door to Grammom Beane's, and my dad drove to a nearby telephone to call the doctor. He then ran to the spring for buckets of water and put them on the gas stove to boil. I remember people standing in the lane waiting for the sound of a crying baby, which finally came around dusk, and Grammom came and told me that I had a baby brother.

A lot of time at the bungalow was spent enjoying swimming and boating. In my baby book it says I was a few weeks old when my parents took me for a ride in the canoe. We used the canoe for many years, and after it wore out my dad bought a small rowboat with an outboard engine. As a growing boy I knew all the trees you could climb and jump off into the creek, I knew all the shallow and deep spots in the creek, and I knew where all the underwater trees were from floaters that had sunk. I still have the locations etched in my memory with a vivid image of the creek.

There were a number of swings on which we could propel out over the creek then let go and drop into the water. We had the best one in the camp that my dad first mounted on a tree in the late twenties. In the late forties it was wearing out, so Grampop Beane somehow got a length of old crane cable from the Reading Railroad shops where he had worked. He showed me how to mount it on a chain loop on a limb, and I then climbed up the Sycamore and mounted it. The cable was about a half inch thick and could have lifted a tank. A stand and ladder were mounted on the adjacent Black Gum tree to give a high start to swing your way out over the water. The swing was still operating in the seventies when the property owners across the creek had it taken down.

There were usually a lot of people around our place on weekends. Grammom and Grampop Beane were next door, and aunts and uncles had bought other nearby bungalows, which made for lots of visits from friends and relatives. Most every Sunday there was a volleyball game on our court. If both men and women played, it was usually courteous, but if it was men only there were no net rules and it could get pretty rough. My dad loved to play well into his seventies and wistfully watched into his eighties. On rainy days we played Pinochle, Parcheesi, Monopoly, or some other game.

Through the years the bungalow underwent a few renovations. A bedroom was added to the north side and a small porch was added in front, which was later turned into a bathroom. My dad, against his thoughts of what a bungalow was meant to be, bowed to "modern" women and installed a shower under the bedroom. But he still washed in the creek until he died long after the shower was installed.

I graduated from Penn State in 1954 and was immediately drafted by the U.S. Army and stationed in Hawaii. When I returned home two years later, I was married and my bride of one year was pregnant. We started regular summer visits to the bungalow and, except for a few years when we lived in Georgia, we spent at least a week each year at the bungalow for over twenty years. As they grew, my four kids enjoyed all the same activities that I had.

After my parents died in 1983, we kept the bungalow for occasional family visits. We built a bathroom with an electric toilet, and in 1985 we replaced the original wooden outhouse with a newer, plastic one. We started holding family reunions in the summer and had get-togethers in the spring and fall that came to be called "The Reading Open." In 1991, with the family becoming older and scattered, we finally sold the bungalow, leaving us all with many wonderful memories of happy and carefree days.

~ Adapted from "When I Was Your Age" by Bill Westley

With my mom in 1956

The Chicken Coop

Elaine Johnson Stefanski

The property where I lived while growing up was one half of a farm from the mid-1800s in Lancaster, NY. Our house had once been the slaughter house/ice house for the farm, and the walls were made of brick that was a foot thick, keeping us warm in the winter and cool in the summer. We had a huge barn out in the center of the property where my father had a workshop on one end and stored his tractor for working up the garden on the other end. He poured a beautiful concrete floor in the middle, room for a car and our bicycles. Behind the barn was a chicken coop where we kept chickens and rabbits throughout the fifties. It was my job to collect the eggs, until one day I accidentally got locked in with the chickens. I was rescued soon enough but relieved of my egg-collecting duties.

In the early sixties things began to change at our house. My father got rid of the tractor and converted that bay into another garage. The chickens and some of the rabbits found their way into the freezer; others were given away. We cleaned out the feathers and straw, took down the partition, put in a pot belly wood stove and fridge, and made our chicken coop into an entertainment center. My brother, now a teenager, formed a band with some of his friends, and the newly renovated coop became their practice stage. Dad gave them some leftover paint and let them create a mural on the wall, and in the summer, instead of complaining about the teenage music being played, the neighbors would sit outside in their chairs to listen. Sometimes Dad and the neighborhood men would play poker out there at a table specially made by my father.

When we started having big picnics on our property, we thought it would be "cool" to rename the chicken coop as "The Bar B Q Pit." So my brother and I made a sign and proudly hung it over the door, but everyone still referred to it as the chicken coop.

On a recent visit to the chicken coop, I was surprised but delighted to see the sign we made still hanging above the door!

Some of my fondest memories are of the many picnics we had with friends, neighbors, and family. Cars would line up on both sides of the driveway on the grass, and the latecomers parked along the road. No one parked in the driveway, because that's where we kids would ride bikes, play games, or fire up

22

my brother's go-kart. We were the post-war baby boomers, so there were lots of cousins my age.

Mom would make ice in the freezer for days, and Dad would take me along to help pick out the flavors of Visniak pop for the parties. We took Mom's metal rinsing tubs out and filled both sides with ice, putting pop in one and beer in the other. Dad would grill hotdogs and hamburgers, and everyone brought a dish to share. In the fall we soaked corn to add to the grill.

1969

After we'd eaten and cleaned up, the tables were taken down or pushed to the side, and Mom got out the record player and put on our square dance records. There was room for two sets on the floor, and as the music played, everyone took turns dancing. Parents helped the children learn the steps to "Duck for the Oyster," Wabash Cannonball," "Marching through Georgia," and many other dances. We all had fun making memories that have lasted a lifetime. My cousins from the city would beg their parents to stay until after dark. Mom would give us glass jars so we could run around trying to catch fireflies, or we would throw water on the lawn and wait for the night crawlers to surface to collect for fishing bait. The picnics never ended until late at night when everyone went home with a smile on their face, and we fell into bed exhausted but with another happy memory.

Summers at our house were full of love and fun. To this day when my brother or I run across friends from our teenage years or out-of-state cousins not often seen, they never fail to mention the fun they remember having at the chicken coop.

From War to Peace

Hilde Smith

Having been born in 1930 in Germany, my early childhood years were happy and carefree. We lived at the edge of a big city, Frankfurt am Main, in a spacious upper flat with an equally spacious backyard. I walked to school and was thrilled that my school was the newest and prettiest. In 1939 I was the flower girl at my sister's wedding and proudly scattered rose pedals along the way into St. Elizabeth Cathedral in Marburg an der Lahn. That summer, celebrating my ninth birthday, I had my first birthday party, which turned out to be the last for many years. I remember my mother canning more than usual that year and explaining that hard times may be coming. That sounded ominous and indeed it was.

Germany was at war soon after. By 1943, bombings of the city had started, and we spent more and more time in the cellar or bunkers. After air raids during the day when families were scattered, I remember running home from school, climbing over rubble, seeing houses on fire, fearing the worst until I was reunited with my Mom and later Dad once he returned from work. At age fifty Dad was drafted, but due to a heart condition he was sent home.

First day of school in 1936

As kids are adjustable, one learned to be part of a water brigade, passing on buckets from a reservoir to fight fires started by the bombs. Phosphor canisters were the worst, as their liquid spread quickly causing new flames everywhere. There was no chance to stop it. One time our neighbor, who lived in the adjoining house next to ours, had to jump out the second floor window to escape after a phosphor canister landed in his house. There was a firewall between the two houses, and as the neighbor's house burned, the firewall became so hot that we had to move all the furniture away from the walls. Certain bombs that we called "mines" created enormous air pressure that blew out windows. My pet parakeet died that way, as I could not take him with me to the shelter. After all the windows were blown out, we boarded them up with cardboard or wood. Another time my dad and a neighbor were up on the roof putting out flames caused by sparks from a neighbor's house. And once a firebomb came in sideways into the attic, where our building manager lived, and got stuck in the bed mattress. My dad ran up to help, and the men picked the bomb up and threw it out the window to the backyard. Fortunately it did not explode; it was a dud.

Children grew up fast under these harrowing circumstances, but we were always thankful to still be alive. We even made a game of collecting shrapnel and parts of detonated bombs that were scattered all over the streets. I had a cigar box full of them and competed heavily with the neighborhood boys as we compared them to see who had the biggest and sharpest pieces. We knew that the jagged metal parts could have killed us if we'd been hit by them, but they became prized trophies as we proudly showed them off.

Eventually the schools were closed. It was not safe for the children to be walking to and from school when there were almost daily bombings. Then the government decided to evacuate all children from the city. We would be sent with our teachers to live in farming villages out in the country where there were no bombings. Taking just a few belongings and leaving our parents behind, my classmates and I, along with our teachers, traveled by train for two to three hours before arriving in the outlying village that was to be our temporary home. The farmers, strangers that we'd never met before, came to pick us up from the train. We'd each been assigned to live with whoever had a spare bed, and I was sent to a household with a daughter who was five years older than me. I worried about my parents back in Frankfurt, but I soon adjusted to my new surroundings. I slept in a straw sack bed above the stables, and at first the cows, shaking their chained heads to chase away the flies, kept me awake. But I eventually became used to that also. Resiliency had become my greatest virtue.

Now that we were safely away from the bombings, we resumed our regular lessons using the village school. We were about fifteen girls with our two teachers, a male and a female, who each taught several subjects. We continued with our studies of German, English and French, as well as Math, Geography, History and Science, but in our meager facility, we did not have any labs. We were a close-knit group; we had grown up together and had been in school together for many years, and we were glad to be back in the classroom studying our lessons.

As most of the men had been drafted into the war, we also spent much of our days working on the farms. It made for a long, full day, and it was hard physical work which we city kids were not used to. I learned how to clean the stables, drive the horse and wagon out to the meadow to help "Grandpa" load the hay, and even managed one time to milk a cow, which, as I remember, was not easy! At first I had so many blisters and sunburn on the back of my knees from bending over to plant potatoes, but it wasn't long before I was as tough as my "big sister." One of the farmers donated a plot of land so we city kids could plant our own garden, and we proudly used our newly acquired farming skills to grow our own produce. We wanted to impress the farmers, and we did. After these busy days I was usually glad to go to bed early, which, in addition to being exhausted, was also necessitated by the electricity black-outs. All lights were kept off at night to prevent being seen by the airplanes flying overhead. Only occasionally did I sit on the window sill to study in the moonlight. I wrote glorious essays about the farmers as the backbone of the country, which I then read to my host family, much to their enjoyment. After listening to my stories they would say, "We are so proud of our Hilde!"

All things considered, life was not too bad except, of course, when the city was bombed. We could see the red sky from the fires and worried about our families. Because there were no phones and no mail, news was hard to get. My Mom came once to visit me by taking the train, which was still running at that time, and then walking to the village. It was hard to see her leave again. But I was fourteen then, and my mother told me, "You can do this," and I did. I grew strong and big from the work and the food that was available to me. Contrary to the shortage in the city, there was no lack of food on the farms, where crops and livestock were plentiful. The government came around to collect the surplus, and the farmers would give them what they had at the time. But city folks, desperate for food to supplement their scanty rations, would also come out with their jewelry, crystal, rugs, and other valuables hoping to trade their belongings for food. After the war I was ashamed to walk next to my mom and dad, who barely weighed a hundred pounds each, and there I was with rosy cheeks, a picture of health. I always worried that people would think I had eaten my parents' rations. Even after the war ended, food remained scarce, and precious items were then exchanged with the Americans for food coupons. It broke my mother's heart to lose some family treasures, but it was either trade or starve. There was a black market for food, and we all participated.

In early 1945, after I had been on the farm for over two years, my dad appeared one day, riding a bicycle because the tires from his car had been taken by the Army. He had a long talk with my teachers and then declared that I was to go with him. I realized soon enough that Frankfurt was already occupied by the American Army, so Dad and I went north towards Marburg, where his sister lived. It took us three days on foot, with my few belongings stowed on the bike. At night we went to the office of the Bürgermeister—the mayor of whatever city we were in—and explained that we were traveling to be with relatives. We asked for shelter for the night, and accommodations were provided for us. We could hear the explosions of bombs as we walked, and when we got to Marburg we learned that my aunt's house had been bombed out. A small note told us where to find her.

So on we went to the next village, where an old widowed woman living alone on a farm had taken in my aunt. My older sister and her child, who had lost everything in an air raid, were there also. We shared one large, long room—four adults, including me, and a four year old. The farmer lady, named Frau Muth, gave us eggs, milk, and butter and shared whatever she could. In return, Dad helped her with the chores, as she was quite old and her sons had all been drafted into the Army. Very soon after our arrival the American Army took over. At first we saw big tanks rolling down the village street with soldiers with bayonets flanking them. I was really scared, but our hostess had hung a long white bed sheet from the upper window, a sign of surrender, and since there were no German soldiers around, the takeover was peaceful. Across from the farm house at the corner was a small inn, which the Army took over and occupied as their base. A dining mess was set up outside, and from the farmhouse we could watch them cook.

We still had Dad's bike, which we rode into town to get our rations, waiting in long lines to receive bread, butter, and eggs. We already had plenty of butter and eggs on the farm, so it was the bread we really wanted. But there often was not enough for everyone in line. We were given cornmeal, but there was no sugar or other baking ingredients, so we used it to make a bland tasting porridge that had to be eaten quickly before it hardened like cement.

One day our much needed, dependable bike was taken from the yard. I saw the thief but could not pursue him, so I ran over to the soldiers and asked them for help. The MP (Military Police) went after the culprit and got our bike back, for which we were so thrilled and thankful. It was our first contact with the Americans, and a day or so later two soldiers showed up at the farm asking to borrow some dishes. I guess they were from a different company and did not have their mess kits with them. Frau Muth complied immediately, and the soldiers brought the dishes back later, nice and clean. On another visit they asked if they could have some fresh eggs from the chickens in exchange for some of their rations. Once again they were successful. Because I was the only one at the farm who could speak English, I acted as the interpreter each time the American soldiers came to the house.

Frau Muth gave us the rations that the soldiers had brought. My sister opened a small can, which was filled with a black powder. She took a spoon to taste it and announced, "Tastes like mocha!" So she had another spoonful, and shortly thereafter her heart started to beat faster. We soon figured out that it had to be "instant coffee," and every one of the adults had their first cup of good coffee in years. We had only had "Ersatzkaffee," an imitation coffee made from chicory that had no caffeine in it. When small children began to gather around the inn-turned-base, the soldiers passed out oranges and

30

chewing gum, which most of them had never seen before, as there was no tropical fruit during the war. At first the kids were scared, especially since they had never seen a black person, but they were often the friendliest and most generous of the soldiers.

After we had been at the farm for several weeks, I looked down the hill one day and saw a very tired woman slowly approaching. I soon realized that it was my mother, and I ran to hug her and hold her tight as tears streamed down my face. She had left the city to come for me, walking because the trains were no longer running, and ended up in a hospital when she collapsed, too weak to go on. Her feet were so blistered they had to be bandaged. When they let her go she continued on to the small village where I had been, only to learn that Dad had picked me up before the Army advanced and that we had gone to Marburg. So she continued on again, a total distance of over seventy miles that took well over a week, until we were finally reunited. That was the happiest moment for me, and tears come to me even now as I write this down.

After regaining some strength, Mom told us that we needed to go back home. Refugees who had been displaced from their own bombed out homes were moving in and occupying every available place, and she was afraid we might lose our home altogether. At that time there was a curfew from dusk to dawn. No one was allowed on the streets, and no one could travel unless they had a permit. Dad had applied for one, but it took time. So the decision was made that he would stay behind, and Mom and I, with use of the one bike, would venture forth. It was a daring undertaking. We had no papers, so we had to keep a low profile, using only country roads and avoiding towns. At night, as Dad and I had done, we would seek out the Bürgermeister of the village we had come to and ask for shelter. We were always welcomed by caring strangers who often shared their food with us.

Days went by before we made it safely to the big city of Frankfurt, which had become an obstacle course. Much of the city had been destroyed and piles of rubble were everywhere.

Army controls surrounded it and there were only a few spots where you could enter the city. Having no travel permits, we approached several trucks on the way, asking if they would hide us among their cargo, and we finally found one willing to do so. We hid towards the front of the truck, crouched between boxes and drums. I was so afraid that I might cough or sneeze when the doors were opened for inspection, but we made it into the city thanks to the friendly trucker.

At long last we arrived at the home that I had been away from for nearly three years, only to find two families occupying our flat. Mother was heartbroken to see how things looked, but we still had a place and squeezed in. Once Dad arrived several weeks later, something had to be done. Everyone was being required to register with the Wohnungsamt, a department overseeing the available living spaces, and we soon learned that with only three in the family, we could not keep our large flat. We were assigned a small flat in a row house further out of town with a bedroom, a living room, a kitchen, and a bath. We took with us what fit into the small place, leaving many things behind, but even then our furniture looked oversized for the tiny apartment. With only one bedroom, I slept in the living room on the couch. Mom mourned losing her home, but we had our own place, no sharing the kitchen and bathroom with two other families. The important thing was that we were together again.

For a year there was no school. The few buildings that were still standing were occupied by the Army. It wasn't until 1946 that efforts were made to find space for the children, and I was assigned to a different school in a new neighborhood. As I hoped to enter the University, I then transferred to a Gymnasium, the equivalent of an American high school plus one year of college, and finished my schooling there. Normally having passed the final exams would give anyone entrance to the University, but there was a "numerus clausus," meaning returning soldiers would be considered first. I was nineteen years old then and just recovering from a serious bout with diphtheria. But after taking the entry exams, I was allowed to start my studies at the Goethe-Universität in Frankfurt.

I focused on English and French with a minor of Political Science, a hot subject at the time being taught by a great visiting professor from the U.S.A. who was well liked and most interesting. My plan was to become a high school teacher of foreign languages. The war was finally over. We still lacked clothing and shoes, but rationing had been lifted, and Mom and Dad finally gained some weight. My sister, widowed after her husband was killed at the Russian front, lived with her aunt for a while until she and my niece got their own place. I took every opportunity to learn the English language more fluently, so I joined an American-German discussion group at the Army Base Chapel. The group was led by the Reverend John Woods, an Army Colonel with a wonderful family, and I babysat for them a few times. The discussion group met on Sunday nights, and it was an uplifting and wonderful learning experience.

In my third year at the Goethe University I applied for a scholarship to study in the U.S.A. After several interviews I was granted one and was asked where in the States I wanted to study. I had no idea, but I had corresponded with a pen pal, Elaine, since 1947 when we were both still in high school. Elaine lived in Chicago, so I thought maybe I would go there and study at the International Institute. But there was no spot available that year, and I was told they would put me in the following year. I was happy to wait, but in July I received an invitation from Keuka College at Keuka Lake in NY. It was a scholarship for the college expenses, partially funded by the Business and Professional Women's Foundation. Unbeknown to me, Reverend Woods had been visited by a former teacher who happened to be the President of Keuka College. In their conversations, foreign students on campus were mentioned, and Reverend Woods immediately mentioned my name as a good candidate.

And so I became a "Keuka girl" for a year! My travel expenses were not included, but when I went back to the University and mentioned that I had accepted this invitation, an American travel grant was issued. By late August of 1951 I was on my way to America. It took ten days on the MS Nelly, a former refugee boat, which was no luxury travel, but we arrived safely in New York. A senior from the college met me at the pier and took me back to her home in New Jersey for the first night. Her lovely Mom, a wonderful hostess, had a small dictionary in her apron pocket and was amazed that I spoke English, even though it was British English in those days. The next day Dottie and I took the train to Geneva then continued on by van to Penn Yan and Keuka Park. I immediately loved the area with the lake and many vineyards, although it was a big change for a former big city girl.

My year there was fantastic, a great exposure to American life, enjoying warm hospitality and meeting and making many new friends. I spent Christmas with the Woods family, who were now living in Baltimore. I felt at home with them and enjoyed being with the children again. In February I came down with the mumps, which required a stay in the infirmary, where I shared a room with another sick student. I met Marilyn's family when they came to visit, and they invited me up to Buffalo for Easter break. It was there that I first met Ray, my future husband, who happened to be Marilyn's brother. I returned to Germany that fall to finish my studies, and Ray kept the mailman very busy.

The following summer, which was 1953, I returned to the U.S. for a visit, and Ray and I got engaged. We were married in Germany during Easter break in 1955, then settled down in Pendleton, NY. When we moved to America, Ray promised my mother that I would come every two years for a visit, a promise that was indeed kept. In 1959 after attending night classes for a year to study American History and Politics, I became a U.S. Citizen. Ironically, the young man who interviewed me for my citizenship asked me more questions about Germany than he did about the United States! I was sworn in at Niagara Falls, and afterward my father-in-law took me to Dairy Queen for a celebratory milkshake.

In addition to our visits to Germany, my parents came to America twice, and my sister and niece visited also. Ray and I eventually had three daughters, who all learned the German language, and I enjoyed a career as a German language teacher. I have many happy memories of our married life of fifty-seven years, and our wonderful girls and their families bring me great joy and comfort now that Ray is gone. I continue to teach German to my friends at the Senior Center, offering free lessons several times a year. I have kept in touch with my German classmates all these years, returning to Germany for reunions and visits. We grew up together during tough times and experienced the hardships of war. But we learned to be strong and appreciate the little things, and we all went on to live happy and productive lives. I love my homeland, but I have found a new home here in America, and I am thankful for the many opportunities it has offered me over the years.

Dressed for my friend Elaine's wedding in 1952.

I Served With Pride

Chuck Fiegl

I received my draft letter in January of 1944, one month after my eighteenth birthday and in the midst of World War II. I had graduated the previous June from Blasdell High School, just outside of Buffalo, where I had served as class president. Most of my classmates were older than me and had already been drafted, so I knew that once I turned eighteen I would also be called to service. The letter from the draft board said that I was to report to the public library in Buffalo for induction.

My family never had a car, so my neighbors drove me downtown. Close to a hundred recruits were there that day to take the oath to serve our country, and I still remember it as if it was yesterday. We stood in front of an officer, raised our right hand, and swore "to bear true allegiance to the United States of America, and to serve them honestly and faithfully, against all their enemies or opposes whatsoever, and to observe and obey the orders of the President of the United States of America, and the orders of the officers appointed over me." As I filled out the paperwork with the enlisting officer, he picked up the stamp marked "Army" and was just about to stamp my paperwork when I asked if I could go in the Navy. He put down the Army stamp, picked up the Navy stamp, and stamped my paperwork. I was told to report to Sampson Naval Training Station in one week to begin basic training. I was so proud and went home to start packing my bags.

One week later my neighbors once again drove me downtown to the Central Terminal. I boarded a train for the first time ever for the nearly three hour trip to Sampson, which was on the east side of Lake Seneca in the Finger Lakes of New York. The train was full of new sailors, some my age and some obviously older. It was around 1:00 in the morning when we arrived at Sampson, and as soon as we got off the train we were lined up to receive the required immunizations, which took several hours. We were then given our uniforms and assigned to our barracks. No time was wasted in starting our training—after a couple hours of sleep, we were up for exercises at 5:30 a.m. We sure knew from the beginning who was in charge. I was one of the youngest at basic training; some of the guys were married and had kids, and I felt sorry for them that they'd had to leave their families. But the war was in full swing and men were needed, so we all had to serve.

Every day started early with an intense physical training regimen: We ran for miles and did lots of calisthenics, always in unison with the other men. Strength and self-discipline were quickly acquired as we worked our bodies more than most of us had ever done before. It was the middle of a bitter cold January, but even with near zero temperatures we reported for exercise in our T-shirts. Normally there would have been water exercises, but it was so cold the lake had frozen over, so that part of the training was left out. Our days were rounded out learning and mastering weapons and gunnery, Morse code, and airplane recognition. If there was any time to be filled, we were assigned to work detail, unloading trucks or working in the mess hall. And there was always more exercise in the afternoon or evening. You didn't have to worry about sleeping at night—we worked so hard all day that sleep usually came as soon as our heads hit the pillows.

There was often some sort of entertainment held in the evening, and I was asked one night to participate in a boxing match. Although I didn't win the match, it was quite memorable because another recruit volunteered to perform some comedy that night. His name was Don Rickles. I never did get to see him, but I still have the program that shows his name following mine.

After completing eight weeks of basic training I was assigned to stay at Sampson for Quartermaster School, which I enjoyed much more than basic training. We were taught to steer a ship, use navigational instruments, and prepare and maintain nautical charts. We also received additional training in Morse code, and I became quite proficient at using the signaling system. Transmitting and interpreting the code would become one of my duties once we were deployed, and it quickly became etched in my memory. Even today, if asked to, I'm pretty sure I could transmit a message in Morse code.

Following Quartermaster School, which lasted another eight weeks, I was sent to the U.S. Naval Amphibious Training Base in Solomons, Maryland. I was assigned to a twenty-four man crew, and we began learning the specifics of the ship we'd be spending the next year on. After this training was complete we headed to New Jersey where our ship was to be commissioned. The LCI 867 was a Landing Craft Infantry, a flat-bottomed, amphibious assault ship that could land troops directly onto beaches. At nearly 168' long and about 24' wide, the LCI 867 was a small ship by Navy standards that could travel around fifteen knots, or seventeen miles, per hour. The blue and gray ship carried twenty-four sailors and four officers but could hold nearly two hundred troops. All ships were given names, and ours, reflecting the total sum of the ship's numbers, was named "Blackjack" after the popular poker game.

In autumn of 1944 Blackjack headed down the Hudson River, and we gradually made our way down the East Coast and travelled through the Panama Canal. Shortly after passing through the canal, we were delayed when one of the officers fell and broke his ankle. I signaled for medical help, and a plane was dispatched to our location. It was nighttime when the plane arrived, so I used light signals to guide the plane to land on the water beside the ship. The officer was taken to Nicaragua, his ankle was attended to, and he was returned to the ship the next day. We then continued up the West Coast to San Diego, arriving just before Christmas. We were given a one week leave, so I hitchhiked to Arizona to visit friends for a few days.

Once we left port again we headed toward the South Pacific. As the captain received our coordinate orders, he would give them to me and I would plot the latitude and longitude on the map and figure out which direction to steer the ship in. I found this to be very interesting, and to this day I still enjoy reading maps. We stopped in Pearl Harbor, where the ship was painted in camouflage colors to better blend with the jungles of the tropics.

The LCI 867
Copyright Navsource.org. Used with permission.

The numbers on the ship then had to be repainted and, as I must have mentioned at one time that I enjoyed my art classes in high school, I was chosen for the project. Secured by a rope, I dangled over the side of the ship each day for nearly a week, meticulously painting the large "867" that identified Blackjack. I've never called myself an artist, but I sure felt like one that week.

After leaving Pearl Harbor we began making our way to the Palau Islands. The chain of islands was mostly under Japanese control, but the U.S. had secured two of the islands in a bloody battle the previous October that had cost many American lives. Twelve American ships were assigned to the area, including Blackjack. It would be our job to patrol and protect the American-held islands, which were being used as airfields for planes as they made their way to Europe, where the ground war was in full force. We worked in rotating shifts aboard Blackjack—four hours on duty then eight hours off. I was usually in the conning tower, the highest point on the ship, receiving and interpreting signals. During the day we used binoculars to watch the Japanese activity. They had set up farms on some of the islands and, ironically, it was those farms that brought on the occasional bout of homesickness. I had spent my summers on my grandmother's farm in Allegany County in the southern tier of New York State, and whenever I heard the crow of roosters from the islands, it reminded me of those carefree days.

At night we circled the islands, shining powerful search lights and watching for any movement. We also kept an eye on the sea and sky for enemy ships and airplanes, using Morse code to communicate with the other ships in our fleet when needed. Although we didn't see any major combat, we came under light fire several times. One time when I was steering the ship the Japanese started shooting at us as we rounded the corner of an island. As I turned the boat to dodge the bullets, I remember thinking, as only a young lad would, that it was like trying to run through the defense on a football field. Fortunately Blackjack did not sustain any major damage in any of these conflicts, and none of our crew was seriously wounded.

We slept in the cramped quarters of the ship's lower level in bunks stacked three high, blanketed by the stifling heat of the tropics. Our food was brought in from Australia, delivered by bigger ships that pulled up alongside Blackjack, and we were lucky to have a talented cook on board who always prepared great meals. We all gained weight because we were eating so well and not getting much exercise on the confines of the ship. Blackjack didn't carry any fresh water for showering, so when it rained we would put out canvas tarps to catch the water, or we'd just lather up and stand out in the rain and wash ourselves. When our clothes needed cleaning we tied them to a rope and threw them overboard, dragging them through the water as the ship moved along. Although they got clean, they also got faded from the saltwater.

After the war ended in August of 1945, we spent several months picking up our fellow servicemen stationed on islands throughout the South Pacific and transported them to bigger ships that would take them back to the States. When we landed on Iwo Jima, we climbed Mount Suribachi where the famous picture was taken of U.S. Marines raising an American flag, and we paid our respects at the cemetery where so many fellow Americans had been buried after losing their lives on Iwo Jima. It was quite an emotional experience that left me with an overwhelming sense of sadness.

Once our assignment in the South Pacific was completed we began the long journey home, once again traveling through the Panama Canal. In Norfolk, Virginia we dropped off Blackjack and switched to an English ship that was headed north, finally arriving in New York City where we would complete our tour of duty and be discharged from the service.

When we got to New York, without any explanation I was assigned to do an overnight watch on the English ship as it sat in the harbor. I had learned in basic training not to question orders, so for my final assignment I boarded the empty ship and spent the night. In the morning I reported back to the base, only to discover that my belongings had been ransacked and my entire uniform and all my badges and memorabilia had been stolen. There was nothing I could do except go out and buy a new uniform just to be discharged in, which cost me $80. My badges and other belongings were never recovered.

After arriving back in Buffalo I enrolled in Brockport College to pursue my lifelong ambition of becoming a Physical Education teacher. Because of my military service I was able to attend college tuition free, which was a great benefit. At Brockport I met my soon-to-be wife Betty, who was also pursuing a degree in education. We were married shortly thereafter and settled down to raise our family in Clarence, NY. I fulfilled my dream of teaching Physical Education, which I did in the Clarence School District for thirty-two years. I also coached football, basketball, and baseball and officiated at swim meets. Betty and I were married for sixty-five years and had four children before Betty's death in 2011.

As a young sailor I served my country with great pride. That sentiment has continued throughout my life and is why I proudly display the American flag outside my home in Clarence.

The Road to America

Athena Alcazaren

From the mountaintop we could see the city below and watched as bombs fell on the churches, the library, and our home. It was 1945 and the majority of the Philippines were back under U.S. control, but in our little pocket of northeastern Luzon, the Japanese held on. San Pablo City was still under attack, and my family had fled to the mountain for safety.

As a politician, my father was being pursued by the Japanese Imperial Army. Many of our relatives had already been killed, including my twenty-three-year-old brother, a First Lieutenant in the Philippine Army, who had been run down by Japanese trucks. This is what we had been told, but his remains were never found, so we were left forever without answers. My grief-stricken mother would take sandwiches to our soldiers returning from the war, hoping to hear news about my brother. But no news ever came.

My parents feared we would all be killed if we did not leave the city. It was decided we would seek shelter with some distant relatives who lived in a small, remote village at the top of a nearby mountain, and word was sent to them to expect our arrival. I was fourteen years old at the time, the thirteenth child of fifteen siblings. Three of my brothers would not go with us; they had already joined the guerrilla Army, fighting with the Americans against the Japanese forces. We would leave in groups of three over the course of several days so as not to raise any suspicion if we were seen.

My father left first with my oldest brother, who was a doctor, and an aide traveled with them. Because he had asthma, it would be a difficult journey for my father, but my brother could give him medicine if he had trouble breathing. Early the next day was my turn. I left with two of my sisters, Libertad, the fourth oldest, who was thirty and knew the way up the mountain, and seven-year-old Polihimnia, who was the youngest. We each wore five or six layers of clothing, which was easier than carrying it all, and took only some water, rice, and sausage to eat along the way. My mother and the rest of my family would leave in the coming days.

In case we were being watched, we started out strolling around a nearby lake as if we were out for a walk, then headed to the next barrio, or neighborhood. After passing through several more barrios we began the long walk up the wooded mountain. The skies were clear and the sun was shining as we made our way up the winding path. We walked all day, stopping occasionally to rest and eat, and arrived at our destination by nightfall, exhausted but happy to see that my father had made it safely ahead of us.

This small village on the mountain was somewhat primitive with very few amenities, but a simple, temporary shelter had been built for us to stay in. My mother and siblings soon joined us, and we began several months of waiting and watching. There was not much to do on the mountain, so we spent a lot of time praying and saying the rosary. My mother was a generous and ambitious woman of great faith, and she did everything she could to keep us strong.

Our greatest enemies on the mountain were the mosquitoes. They were everywhere and attacked us relentlessly day and night. Eventually we all became sick with malaria. We had no access to the proper medicine, so there was nothing we could do. Many days we shook and trembled with fever and chills. After several months we were finally rescued by guerrilla soldiers working under General MacArthur, who escorted us down the mountain.

Because our home had been destroyed, we were taken to the town of Pila, Laguna, about fifteen miles north of San Pablo, where arrangements had been made for a house that we could live in. We were so very grateful to have this new home after all that we had been through and spent a few more months regaining our health and becoming adjusted to our new life.

High school graduation

Eventually I finished high school and attended college, graduating magna cum laude from the University of the East with a degree in orthodontics. At first I had wanted to be a nurse, but my mother said, "No, you are too smart...you will become a doctor." Fortunately, as an only child, my mother had received an inheritance that helped us to rebuild our lives after losing our home and also allowed us all to receive a good education.

After receiving my degree I was given a scholarship to attend Tufts University in Massachusetts for my post-graduate studies, which included a three-year residency at Forsyth Dental Infirmary. I then returned to the Philippines fully trained as an orthodontist. Part of my scholarship terms had been that I would join the faculty at the University of the East, which I did for thirty-five years, teaching in the mornings and practicing orthodontics in the afternoons. I also met my future husband, who was a professor of prosthodontics, at the University. We were married in 1957 and eventually had four children.

With my daughter at her Kindergarten graduation

Many times over the years we were encouraged by our children to move to America. But my husband was very involved in dental politics in the Philippines and had no desire to do so. However, shortly after his sudden death in 2004, I had a terrifying experience that finally brought me to America for good.

I had walked to a nearby bank to withdraw some money and was on my way back home. As I passed a gas station I was approached by a woman who claimed she was a former patient and said she wanted to introduce me to her husband, who was in a nearby car. I walked over to the car with her, but when we got there I was forced to hand over my purse with my money and all the jewelry I was wearing. I was very frightened and went to the police, but my money and jewelry were gone.

After this happened, my children convinced me to move to America to live with my sister. I was sad to leave my home and country, but I was also very happy because three of my children already lived in America. I stayed with my sister, Polihimnia—whom I had climbed the mountain with so many years before—for nearly eight years. Now a psychiatrist, she helped me to deal with the fear that had remained with me since the incident at the gas station. When my sister herself became ill, I went to live with my daughter in Missouri for a year before coming to live with my son in Buffalo. It was in 2012, while living with my daughter, that I finally and proudly became a citizen of The United States of America.

Life in Youngstown...and Beyond

Marge McMillen

December 7, 1941 occurred just more than a week past my ninth birthday. I remember listening to the radio and hearing President Franklin D. Roosevelt's booming voice recount the surprise attack by the Japanese at Pearl Harbor, and I was further shocked to hear that the U.S. was now at war. My father, who had left us the year before, had already joined the U.S. Army, but because of the attack, he was not discharged as planned. He instead was kept in service and sent to Australia, where he would spend the entire duration of WWII serving as a medic.

My mother was dating a baker by the name of Andy Kmets. He was drafted and sent to Fort Niagara in Youngstown, NY, where he would serve the entire war years as head baker. Actually, at one point he had been sent overseas to fight but was brought home when it was discovered that his two brothers had just been killed within one week of each other at Normandy. Although all enlisted men slept in fully-occupied barracks, Andy, as head baker, slept in a single bedroom that was part of the bakery, with another bedroom that was occupied by Andy's two helpers. I doubt if anyone was jealous of these three men since no one in their right mind would relish the idea of having to get up at 3:00 a.m. every day to start baking items needed for breakfast.

Mom and I moved from our home in Buffalo to Youngstown, a small village in the northwest corner of the state where the Niagara River empties into Lake Ontario. We rented an old farm house on Second Avenue that consisted of three bedrooms upstairs and a living room, dining room, kitchen, and a spare room downstairs. For reasons unknown to us, someone had left an old upright piano in the spare room. We haughtily named this room The Music Room, and I took piano lessons from a lady down the street for the exorbitant price of fifty cents an hour. The only heat was from an oil stove in the living room and a coal stove in the kitchen, both of which were banked at night. We slept upstairs where there was NO heat. I would wake in the morning under piles of thick comforters and blow huge puffs of frosty breath into the air. I'd grab the clothes I had set out the night before and run down the stairs to the only room in the house that was warm, the bathroom, where a gas water heater located behind a closed door would fend off the freezing cold occupying the rest of the house.

Mom obtained a job as secretary to the lieutenant in charge of the PX (Post Exchange) at Fort Niagara, and as a result, I was given a pass that allowed me to enter the fort anytime I wanted to. I was, in fact, the only child I knew in all of Youngstown that was allowed to do that. I would walk the tree-lined streets of Youngstown, approach the MP's guard house that was situated at the fort's gate, show my pass and be waved on. As an aside, we had no car, so Mom and I walked everywhere unless we were headed to Niagara Falls, and then we would take a bus.

I have wonderful memories of eating at the PX on the base, where the thick hamburgers would put McDonalds to shame and the milkshakes were made with real ice cream and were thick and delicious. I always put a nickel into the juke box, choosing my favorite song, which was either a Glen Miller piece or Jose Iturbi playing Chopin's Polonaise. Mom and I would then meet Andy and go to the movie on base at a cost of ten cents. Andy did, just once, get permission for Mom and me to eat in the mess hall. I can't remember what we had, but I remember the food was good. Another time he got tickets for us to see a live show on base with none other than Bob Hope as the star.

In time, German prisoners of war were kept on Fort Niagara grounds. The POWs were housed in the same type of barracks and ate the same food, including Andy's bread and baked goods, as did all the American soldiers stationed at Fort Niagara. In fact, the POWs actually had it so good that many fought to return to the United States after the war. In the summer, my friends and I would walk on the highway that led to our favorite swimming spot in Lake Ontario, where we had to pass the barbed-wire topped chain-linked fence that surrounded the POW compound. The young German prisoners would be sitting outside their barracks, and they would do what all young men did in those days when they saw young girls...they'd whistle at us. I was wearing lipstick then and looked much older than my eleven or twelve years of age, and though I knew these were the enemies, you can see how it went to my head. Many of the trusted POWs worked on local farms, but a few of them were allowed to work at the PX, and they became friends of my Mom. Anytime I would arrive to meet her for dinner and a show, they would all greet me with their heavily accented English. One of them crafted a wooden bowl and gave it to my mother, a treasure that is now in my possession. I assure you, it was World War II and I hated the Nazis, but it was difficult to think of these young German soldiers as the enemy.

There was only one school in Youngstown consisting of grades Kindergarten through 12th grade, and I attended the 5th, 6th and 7th grades there. The school, known as "The Red School House," now houses artifacts from the 1940s. Today what was once Fort Niagara is now a public park with only a few buildings left from the WWII Fort Niagara. One of them is the Officer's Club, which contains a painting on the wall done by a German POW, and the other is one of the officers' duplex homes that stood along the banks of the Niagara River. It looks exactly like the one my mother's boss, Lieutenant McMann, lived in. I used to babysit his two children in that very same home, or one identical to it. I remember one particular evening when he and his wife had a party and asked me to stay upstairs where their children were sleeping in case one should wake up. I spent the evening reading a book in the senior McMann's bedroom, and I remember Mrs. McMann bringing me up a tray of snacks, which I thought was very kind of her to do. The tray consisted of cheese and crackers, fruit, and...caviar. I have since found out how much it costs, so I can safely say it was lucky for both my mother and me that I absolutely hated it.

As a young girl in Youngstown

Andy and I maintained a Victory Garden in the empty lot next to our house, and I loved every minute of it. I even joined the 4-H Club and raised rabbits and a lamb in the adjacent barn. I must confess, however, that even though I am an avid animal lover, this did get to be more work than fun, and I wasn't too disappointed when Mom sold some and gave the rest to the SPCA. There was a great fishing spot in Lake Ontario on the north end of the fort, and Mom and I would fish for blue pike (now extinct), then walk back through Youngstown, where we would have the fish filleted, then arrive home to eat these truly fresh morsels. You've never tasted fish so good!

After the war my father returned home sick with malaria. An already thin man, he was now skin and bones. He went back to work at his former place of employment, The Buffalo Hospital for the Insane on Forest Avenue, where he met Addie, a nurse who would become his second wife. Mom and Andy married also. I lived with Mom and Andy in Kenmore, but now had four parents...all of whom I loved and all of whom seemed to love me back. I considered myself very lucky.

I met my future husband on a blind date while in high school. In spite of the fact that I had a botched hair color job at the time and was wearing a scarf around my head, we hit it off and continued to date all through high school. The Korean War was in full force after Bob graduated, and rather than being drafted into the Army, he joined the Air Force. I went to work as secretary to the principal of Roosevelt School in Kenmore and didn't see Bob for two years. By a strange twist of fate, he was transferred to Lockport, not too far from Kenmore, and we started dating again. We were married in 1952. Six months after our wedding, the Air Force sent Bob to Labrador, and I took a job as a secretary at Linde Air, renting an upstairs apartment in Kenmore until he was discharged.

When Bob returned home from Labrador and received an honorable discharge, he was offered a job with Canadian Marconi. We moved to Montreal, Quebec for six weeks, then St. Johns, Newfoundland, where we would spend the next year. Our first baby, Melonie Dawn, was born there in 1955. She was a beautiful baby who died only sixteen months later at Children's Hospital in Buffalo at the hands of an inept resident doctor. After our return to the states, Bob went to work for Motorola, and we were blessed with two more children, Rob and Lori, who were born respectively in 1957 and 1959 at the same Children's Hospital in Buffalo. As the children grew, Bob's job took us to Rochester for a time and then New Jersey, where we lived until moving back to Buffalo when Bob retired.

Our two children are grown and married and have given us four grandchildren and five great-grandchildren, all of whom are loves of our lives. One of the more pleasant things we've been able to do in retirement is travel. We've been lucky enough to see a large majority of the United States and have visited many countries of the world. We are still enjoying life, though not quite as varied or as fast. Knowing my love of dance, Bob suggested I join the dance classes at our Senior Center, which I did, enrolling in a lyrical jazz class. I've been doing that for twenty years now, and STILL enjoy every minute of it. We both play bridge, and I've taken up writing as a hobby, which has been very satisfying and rewarding. I have self-published six books so far and am working on my seventh!

Like everyone else, we've hit some bumps along life's journey, but all in all, we've enjoyed our stay on this earth and look forward to what life has to offer us in whatever amount of years we are destined to live.

Green Beret

Ron Butler

In 1963, hoping to broaden my career opportunities, I enlisted in the United States Army. I had lived in Buffalo my whole life and attended Burgard Vocational High School, where I played football and tennis and studied commercial printing. I'd also taught myself Morse code and spent many years as a licensed ham radio operator, a popular hobby in those days. I had been working in the printing trade since graduating from high school five years earlier, but after being laid off several times, I set my sights on the military. I was twenty-three years old and was not aware of the conflict in Vietnam. I was an only child, and my mother, with thoughts of World War II and the Korean War still fresh in her memory, was not happy—to say the least—that I had enlisted. On July 23 I left home for Fort Dix, New Jersey. It was not an easy departure.

During basic training we were given a battery of tests to determine our skills and knowledge in a variety of areas from automotive and electrical to communication and medical. At the end of basic training, with my mother in attendance, I was assigned to another eight weeks of rigorous infantry training, during which I signed up to be a paratrooper. Before I left for jump school in Fort Benning, GA, I was called to an interview with a couple officers, who asked if I would want to go to Special Forces training. At the time I had no idea what "special forces" were, but because I had done well on all my testing and had a background in Morse code, I met the initial qualifications and agreed to the training. I completed jump school, earning my Airborne Wings, and then after a thorough personal background search performed by the U.S. Army, I was selected for entry into the Special Forces Training Group located at Fort Bragg, North Carolina.

Activated specifically for Vietnam, which initially we didn't know, the Special Forces provided extensive training in communications, medical theory, weaponry, and survival. Our skills were rehearsed in Pisgah National Forest in the Appalachian Mountains of North Carolina as we jumped from planes and practiced using explosives. One day I saw a small sign outside the officers' room which read: "Those who want to volunteer for the Republic of Vietnam, come in and sign up." It was the first I'd heard of Vietnam. Since I was still in training, I didn't sign up and didn't think any more about it. After eight rigorous and demanding months, I proudly won my Green Beret and became a member of America's elite 5th Special Forces.

Following another lengthy interview, I was assigned to a twelve-man A-Team made up of specialists in combat demolition, communications, medical, operations and intelligence, and light and heavy weaponry. I was a communications specialist, but each man was cross-trained in all areas. By this time we knew we were headed to Vietnam. There was no voluntary sign-up done—as Special Forces, we had been trained for this purpose. The conflict in Vietnam was now widely known and widely unpopular, and there was much unrest in the country because of it. But we'd been told we were going to fight the spread of communism, and as highly trained soldiers, we believed in what we were doing. At the time, I thought the public would eventually understand and support our mission.

A key part of our training then took place. A large compound at Fort Bragg had been created to simulate our destination in Vietnam. Enclosed in concertina wire—long coils of barbed wire—as the bases in Vietnam would be, the compound contained two barracks, and we spent about thirty days within the compound studying maps and going over exactly what we'd be doing in Vietnam. In November of 1964 our A-team, along with two officers, left for Vietnam. We flew from Fort Bragg to Chicago, then to San Francisco, where we boarded a commercial plane headed to Hawaii. Because of the unrest and the war protests that had begun, we were instructed to stay in our civilian clothes to avoid any confrontations with protesters. In Hawaii we donned our uniforms and switched to a military plane.

We landed in Da Nang, Vietnam, spending a week there before continuing to Pleiku. I was assigned to Bravo 20 as Staff Sergeant with the duties of training the First Cavalry in air assault techniques. On February 7, 1965, three months after our arrival and during Tet (the Vietnamese New Year), the Viet Cong, carrying satchel explosives, overran the base. Thirty helicopters and eleven men were lost. For most of the troops this was our first combat experience and our initiation into war. It was when everything we had trained for became all too real. Fortunately, none of the men on our A-team was seriously injured. From my position on top of a communications bunker, I did suffer several facial and scalp wounds caused by an exploding sixty millimeter mortar round. My wounds were treated on base, although I still have a scar above my left eye, and I eventually received a Bronze Star and a Purple Heart Medal for this injury.

Two weeks later Bravo 20 left for Nha Trang where, with the help of interpreters, we trained Vietnamese rangers in parachuting and air assault. As a sign of camaraderie, we traded Jump Wings after jumping together, giving them American insignias for their Vietnamese insignias. After thirteen months in Vietnam, which was the standard tour of duty at that time, we were scheduled to be relieved and sent home. But the airplane carrying our replacements experienced mechanical failure after leaving Hawaii and went down in the Pacific Ocean. The entire crew was lost. We were asked to stay another thirteen months and all agreed to do so.

Our next stop was Plei Me where, again working with interpreters, we began preparing the Montagnard—the native mountain people—to protect their villages. Army medics worked with the women and children, and we trained the men on weapons. Surplus rifles from World War II had been sent over for this purpose, which, as the Motagnard were small people and the rifles were long and bulky, was not an easy task. Although we mainly prepared them to defend against the Viet Cong, the Montagnard also at times had to ward off the South Vietnamese, who saw them as an inferior people and would try to take their money and belongings from them.

One night at Plei Me, at 3:00 a.m. and during a rainstorm, the Viet Cong 141st Battalion struck. Although the compound was surrounded by concertina wire and mines, there were so many of them that, despite some of their troops being killed by the mines, they were able to enter the compound and overtake us. We had been trained to stay awake at night and sleep during the day, especially during inclement weather, as that was when attacks would most likely happen. But there were only twenty of us on the base, along with the Viet Rangers and Montagnard. We were gravely outnumbered and called for helicopters to evacuate. There was confusion, however, because our commander, named Moore, was away at a nearby base for a meeting of the top brass, and that base, also under the command of an official named Moore, was also attacked that night. Eventually helicopters arrived as five Viet Rangers and I continued to return fire, allowing the Montagnards and other Viet Rangers to evacuate the area before departing ourselves. Several Americans, including three men of our A-team, were killed that night, and the camp was rendered temporarily useless. Honoring our commitment to "leave no man behind," we eventually went back to Plei Me and retrieved the remains of our fallen comrades to be returned to the U.S. The loss was hard; we had worked together as a twelve-man team for over a year and had been like brothers. I was awarded a Silver Star Medal, the third highest military decoration, for my actions at Plei Me.

My next assignment was C/2 Mike Force in Pleiku. I coordinated the Viet Rangers defense of nine Special Forces Camps and a base housing a helicopter assault force. While at Pleiku, still believing that our mission was necessary and justified, I re-enlisted for another three years. Shortly afterward we received word of a location in Cambodia where American POWs were being held, and we were given orders to attempt a rescue. An assault team was assembled and we unofficially crossed the border via helicopters into Cambodia in search of the prisoners. Unfortunately the Viet Cong had learned of the rescue mission and vacated the area, leaving the effort unsuccessful. Because we had to notify the Vietnamese Army of all our planned maneuvers, it was not known who the informant had been.

In January, 1967 I completed my duties in Vietnam and received the Vietnam Cross of Gallantry, the Vietnamese

Campaign Ribbon, and a Good Conduct Medal before leaving Pleiku. After a thirty day leave I would be stationed in Germany. Traveling again through San Francisco and Chicago, I arrived in Buffalo and found war protests everywhere, especially on the college campuses. We had heard that public opposition to the war had continued to grow, but I had not been prepared for the intensity of protesting that was occurring. With all the demonstrations, marches, and rallies, I could not venture far from home. Even though I stayed in my civilian clothes, again to avoid confrontation, my military haircut obviously identified me as a soldier. After deciding to end my leave early, I did not put my uniform on again until I reached Fort Dix, from where I then flew to Germany.

I arrived in Bad Tolz, Germany assigned to Company A, 10th Special Forces. Company A participated in maneuvers with the German and Austrian NATO Forces, which included both ski and parachute exercises. I completed my tour of duty in Germany working in communications for the U.S. Armed Forces Europe Radio Network. The powerful radios were in a secure site and used to transmit coded messages throughout Europe. We would receive the code and pass it on to our captain for interpretation. I did not see any more combat while serving in Germany for the next two and a half years.

On July 24, 1969 I was honorably discharged from the United States Army as a Sergeant Major. I had enlisted in 1963 with the intention of serving one term, but I had been pulled deeper and deeper into military life through my training and immersion in the war. There were no welcome home parades, no yellow ribbons tied around trees. It was easy to be resentful. I had done what the soldiers and sailors before us had done—fought for freedom and security. I had served our country for over six years, but it took much longer to settle back into civilian life. I lived in Los Angeles for a while, where I attended college and earned a diploma. Then for the next fifteen years I travelled the country, finding jobs in the print industry as I moved from city to city. Sometimes solitude can be ones greatest healer. In 1984 I returned to Buffalo to help care for my ailing mother and met my wife Jean. We married in 1985 and raised four children together—Gregg, Lynn, Bobby, and Jennifer.

I have remained active with the Niagara Frontier Chapter of the 82nd Airborne Division Association, attending various ceremonies and services, marching in parades, and serving as a pallbearer at the funerals of fellow veterans. Although not the original, I still wear my 5th Special Forces uniform, with the now obsolete South Vietnamese wings among my decorations. And I still wear my Green Beret with pride. I am a Vietnam Veteran.

Armed Forces Day in May of 2015

The Wreath

Bernadine Ginter

In August of 2004 I embarked on what would be my last of many wonderful trips to France. Travelling alone from LaGuardia Airport in New York City, I met up with my tour group after landing in Marseille. We had all come to France for the same purpose—to mark the 60th Anniversary of the invasion of southern France by the Allied forces in World War II. The group was made up of both American and French WWII veterans, their wives, and, as in my case, several widows of veterans. For the next two weeks we would retrace the route of the invasion as we traveled through southern France by bus, stopping to visit some of the momentous and historical sites along the way.

My husband, Andrew, had been part of the U.S. Army 3rd Infantry Division, serving with Audie Murphy, one of the most decorated American soldiers of WWII. They had fought through North Africa, Sicily, Italy, France, Germany, and Austria for nearly a year and a half, liberating both Rome and Paris from Nazi control, but at a heavy cost of life. During the invasion of southern France, the 3rd Division had been attached to the French 1st Army, and the two divisions had formed close bonds that continued well after the long and brutal war.

Andrew Ginter

Andrew and I first attended a reunion of the Society of the 3rd Infantry in North Carolina in the early seventies. Through the Rhine and Danube Association, veterans of the French 1st Army had also been invited, several of whom attended then invited the 3rd Division to their reunion in Paris the following year. We attended the yearly 3rd Division reunions, which were held in various cities throughout the United States, for the next twenty years, and we attended the Rhine-Danube reunions in France every few years. Our European travel was usually extended to two or three weeks, sometimes with others from the reunions and sometimes on our own. Although much of our travel was dedicated to the poignant remembrance of war, the reunions allowed us to stay connected to Andrew's comrades, many of whom became lifelong friends, and also provided us opportunities to visit many interesting and historical places.

In 1974 we made our first visit to Italy. Aside from the good food and romantic atmosphere, we were there for the

30th Anniversary of the invasion of Anzio by the Allied forces. In that horrific four month battle dominated by the Germans, the 3rd Division had suffered many losses before a final victory. Many of Andrew's comrades were buried at the Sicily-Rome American cemetery in Nettuno. Nearly 8000 Americans who gave their lives in WWII are laid to rest in the beautiful seventy-seven acre cemetery, and the names of more than 3000 listed as missing in action are memorialized on the walls of the chapel. My husband struggled with his emotions as he gazed out at the sea of white marble crosses marking the graves, saying later that it was the most emotional thing he'd ever done.

We returned to Nettuno in both 1984 and 1994 to mark the 40th and 50th Anniversaries with ceremonies attended by hundreds of veterans and their families. Both the President of Italy, Oscar Luigi Scalfaro, and U.S. President Bill Clinton spoke at the 50th Anniversary before placing a wreath at the memorial. Afterward President Clinton and his wife hosted a reception for the veterans and their families.

In 1994, after attending the ceremonies in Anzio and Nettuno in June, we returned to Paris in August for the 50th Anniversary of the invasion of southern France. Operation Dragoon, as it was called, was launched on August 15, 1944, Andrew's twentieth birthday and two months after the Normandy landing. It had been a much larger attack than Anzio and lasted only a month before liberating Paris and the south of France, but many lives were again lost. Andrew had been seriously wounded during a battle in the town of Artenia. His life was saved by a young medic named Joseph McElroy, who later lost his own life. 860 Americans are buried in the Rhone American Cemetery in Draguignon, and their sacrifice was recalled at the ceremony as a wreath was placed at the memorial by the widow of the French 1st Army General Jean de Lattre de Tassigny.

Through the years our overseas travel also took us to Rome, Austria, and Germany, as well as many other cities throughout France. We went on a Mediterranean Cruise with the French Veterans; we visited the grave site of the Revolutionary War hero General Lafayette at the garden of the Picpus, and we were in Paris the night Jacques Chirac was elected President of France. We were invited to attend the victory reception at the Hotel de Ville and somehow, in the throngs of people, I ended up standing just feet away from him as he gave his victory speech.

Unfortunately, Andrew developed serious health problems and passed away in 1997. I struggled with the loss and decided to honor his memory by continuing to attend the reunions of the 3rd Infantry Division, and I also made several more trips to Europe. After first returning in 2002, I went for the 60th reunion in 2004. It was good to be with others who shared this unique bond. As we made our way around southern France we spent a day on the Rhine River on a French aircraft carrier, and we toured a museum dedicated to the 3rd Infantry. We also visited the site in Holtzwihr where a memorial had been erected marking the spot where Audie Murphy had mounted a tank and single-handedly launched an attack against the Germans, allowing his men to retreat.

A group of French reenactors dressed in WWII uniforms of American soldiers accompanied the tour and participated in the memorial services. In each city that we stopped in along the way, we were welcomed by the mayor with a warm reception and champagne. There were several luncheons honoring the veterans, with an empty table set to represent the fallen and unknown soldiers. In spite of the nostalgia, there was good friendship and camaraderie among the group, and we enjoyed our time together.

The tour, of course, included a ceremony at the Rhone American cemetery to once again honor the sacrifice of those who had lost their lives. On this final visit I was able to find the grave of the young medic who had saved my husband's life in Operation Dragoon. And I was stunned but thrilled when I was asked, along with one of the veterans, to lay the wreath at the 60th Anniversary memorial ceremony. The widow of General de Lattre de Tassigny, who had laid the wreath for many years, had died the previous year at the age of ninety-six. As the veteran and I placed the wreath on the memorial, it was announced that I was the widow of Andrew Ginter, a brave and gallant soldier. It was such an honor and privilege and a fitting culmination to many years of paying my respect to the fallen soldiers of World War II.

With the memorial wreath at the Rhone American cemetery

Remembering TaTa

Latif Alam

"I believe that when we die, God will ask what we have done in the world. He won't ask how much money we made, or what kind of car we drove, or how big our house was. He will ask how we treated other people and how many people we helped."

I was born in South India. Our country was an independent state separate from India which, at that time, was under British rule. We had our own culture, our own language, our own currency, and our own King. The King was a wealthy man, and he took care of his country and his people. Education was important and provided to all children—boys and girls—right through college.

As the first-born of seven children, I helped my mother care for my siblings. We were three girls and four boys separated by twelve years. My father, a professor of geography, was an intelligent man and devoted to his family. We were happy, and life was good.

When I was about eight or nine years old, one of my brothers found a puppy in the street and brought him home. My youngest brother at the time was only a year old and could not yet speak clearly. Whenever he saw the little dog he would excitedly say "TaTa TaTa TaTa," over and over, so "TaTa" became our puppy's name. A gold-colored dog with brown patches and big, shiny eyes, TaTa was a playful puppy who quickly became part of the family and almost as quickly grew to be a big dog. He was a loving, protective dog, and he was very smart. He could sense our feelings, and we could tell by looking into his eyes that he understood us. We all loved TaTa very much, and he loved us. He was our constant companion.

As girls, my sisters and I were not allowed to play outside on our own. Even when we went to school, which was separate from the boys, we were picked up in a cart pulled by two bulls, and a curtain was held up for us to walk behind as we went from the door to the cart. At the time, we thought nothing of this. It was customary and expected.

Because we were not allowed to play outside, we could not easily stay in touch with our cousins, who lived three miles away with my grandparents. So we trained TaTa to deliver messages back and forth. We would write a note and tie it around TaTa's neck and tell him to take it to our cousins, and he did. He even knew that my grandfather was not too fond of him, so he would go to the back entry to my cousins' room to avoid grandfather, pawing at the door to let them know he was there. Then he would wait for the reply note to be written and tied back around his neck before running home.

When we went for carriage rides TaTa would trot along beside the carriage. He barked at any boys or men who came near us, except my brothers, letting them know that he was there to protect us. And when we went to the movies, held in big, circus-like tents, TaTa would go too, sitting beside us and watching the movie. Of course he barked if any young men appeared in the movie.

TaTa also learned to help my brothers. If they were playing outside and he sensed that they needed him, he would run like a bullet to their side. One of the favorite pastimes of my brothers was kite fighting, a popular sport in India. The boys would coat their kite stings with glue and powdered glass and then try to cut each other's kites down from the sky. Part of the competition was trying to capture any kite that was cut down. All the boys who were not flying the kites would start running as soon as a kite went down, racing to be the first to reach the downed kite. But TaTa could outrun them all, and he became one of the best kite runners at the competitions!

Yes, TaTa was a part of our family, and he did not like to be away from us. Once we went on a vacation and TaTa had to stay with my grandparents. He missed us very much and would not eat while he was away from us. He was so very happy to see us when we returned.

When I was fourteen years old, my mother, who we called Ammani, became ill with jaundice and was hospitalized. Back then in India dogs roamed freely, so TaTa, who loved Ammani very much, came to my mother's hospital room with us. He seemed to know that Ammani was very sick, and he would not leave her. He stayed at the hospital, sleeping under the bed at night, and we brought his food and water to him. The nurses did not mind and worked around him, but we had to take TaTa out of the room when the doctors came in, because, as usual, he barked at any men.

After she had been in the hospital for about a week, my mother was given the wrong injection, which caused her death.

She was just thirty-five years old. Like all of us, TaTa was devastated, and he barked and cried when Ammani died. Afterward he became even more protective of us children, taking on a motherly role. He looked after us constantly and even barked for us to come in when it was time for dinner.

In 1947, one year after my mother died, my father decided to move our family to Pakistan. Relatives were pressuring him to remarry so that he would have help caring for his children. But he did not want to remarry, nor did he want anyone else to raise us. It was also at this time that turmoil had begun in South India. The British rule of India had ended with the Partition of India, and millions of people were crossing the borders between India and the newly formed countries of East and West Pakistan. There was much violence against women and children, and fighting between religious extremists escalated.

We packed what belongings we could and left our home in South India. Because we were traveling by train, father decided we had to leave TaTa with my grandparents. We were so sad to leave him behind. But as we began our train ride we looked out the window, and there was TaTa running along beside the train. My father pulled the cord to stop the train then went to the conductor and asked if we could bring TaTa on board. The conductor said we would have to buy him a ticket, which my father did, and TaTa happily joined us on the train. When we reached Bombay, we had to switch trains. The city was very crowded and there was much commotion as we waited for our transfer. In the confusion, my three year old brother wandered off. We began searching frantically for him, but it was TaTa who found him and brought him back.

We traveled for two days and one night by train. Then, because we had no passports, we got off the train and walked two more miles to the border through an area known as "No Man's Land." When we finally reached the border, the guards would not allow us to bring TaTa info Pakistan. We were devastated. One of the guards told my father we could take TaTa if he gave them one of his daughters, which of course my father refused to do. We were forced to go on without our beloved TaTa. We cried and cried as we walked on, listening to the sound of TaTa barking behind us. To this day I get tears in my eyes thinking about him and wondering what became of him.

And so we began our new life in a new country without our mother and without TaTa. But my father taught us that if we were good and if we lived a life of helping others, we would one day be reunited with them. He taught us that money was immaterial and that education was important. This became our guiding principle, and my sisters and I all became doctors so that we could help others. And all of us committed ourselves to being good so that someday we will reach heaven and once again see Mother and TaTa.

A New Country

Myrth Roalsvig

In 1953, spring was in the air in Norway, and my husband Jan Per was about to graduate from Oslo University with a degree in physics. He had been an excellent student and, in addition to physics, was qualified to teach math or science in any high school. But there were no jobs available, unless we would move to northern Norway and live in a barrack. It had been almost a decade since the five years of German occupation had ended, but the country still had not been able to catch up with demands for housing. People were sharing houses and apartments. We had been married for about a year and had just had a baby, but we were still living with my parents.

One day we saw a letter posted on a bulletin board at Oslo University: "Dr. William Haslam at Saskatchewan University in Saskatoon, Canada is looking for a qualified graduate student to do research on gamma rays from a Betatron, work that could lead to a Ph.D. in about three years." With a little push from his wife, Jan Per decided to give it a try. He wrote a letter stating that he would like to do the research but also explaining that he was married and a new father and could not afford such a long trip.

The return letter from Dr. Haslam arrived shortly thereafter and brought good news. He wanted us to come as soon as possible, wife, baby and all; the trip across the ocean would be fully paid for by the university. He would arrange for a place for us to stay in Saskatoon, and he suggested a certain pay per month which we thought we easily could survive on. We would be gone for three years, but our families understood that it was a great opportunity; with a Ph.D., Jan Per would be able to get a good job when we returned.

It was quite a trip. First we traveled aboard a Norwegian ship over the North Sea from our hometown of Stavanger to Newcastle, England, then took the train to Liverpool for a one night stay. Because of the coal industry, Liverpool was a dirty city, and we had to shake soot off the pillows before going to bed at night. The baby was sleeping in his new buggy and, thankfully, was never a problem. In the morning we breakfasted with a tweed clad gentleman who ordered hot oatmeal cereal with a fried egg and raspberry jam on top, a small detail that I've always remembered because I'd never before seen anyone put an egg on their oatmeal!

In Liverpool we boarded the ocean liner Arcadia, which had the most inexpensive fare we could find. Even though the University was paying our way, we traveled as frugally as we could. It was a very old ship that we learned was going to be cut up the following month. To us the boat was huge, with first and second class accommodations as well as third class, where we were. First class was wired off from the rest of the passengers; the higher decks were reserved for the rich and mighty. It was strange to hear only English spoken around us all day. We had not been very concerned about the language since we both had taken years of English classes in school and read it easily. But this was different. I knew I had to learn to speak English quickly, partly because of the needs of the baby, so I tried my best. People often smiled, but very few made fun of my efforts. Jan Per just decided to stay silent. I had a very good time and enjoyed the journey and all the different people I met.

When we arrived in Montréal after nine days at sea, I had my first lesson in English snobbery. In Norway we had always been used to "ladies and children first," but when we disembarked in hot 90° weather wearing wool coats and hats with a screaming, hungry baby, I found out that policy did not apply on an English boat. We would have to wait several hours while first and second class left the ship before it would be our turn. All my pleas to the captain were ignored. We did not count. We were only third class. As a final insult, my beautiful new wool hat shrunk in the stifling heat; it would never fit again.

After what seemed like forever, it was finally our turn. We were so happy to see my parents' friends standing in the crowd on the dock calling to us in Norwegian "Velkommen to Canada!" Arrangements had been made to spend a few days with them before continuing on to Saskatoon. After our long journey on the rickety ship, it was great to be in a house again and to have toast jumping up at us for breakfast. This was something new! We never used toasters at home. Our friends helped us a few days later catch the train to Saskatoon. This train ride was quite interesting. We had been riding trains in Norway both during the day and at night and were familiar with the little cabins with built-in washbasins and toilets. But on this train we slept in bunk beds separated only by a curtain and had to share washbasins with many others. With people snoring and whistling behind the curtains, it was difficult to catch any sleep that night.

When the door was opened the next day and we looked out at our destination, we felt like we'd landed on another planet. Yellow wheat on tall stems was waving in the wind all around us. Not a hill, not a single tree, just yellow wheat. Far away we could see a tall, three-story shed, intended to keep the wheat, we later learned.

A group of people from the University had come to meet us at the little train station. After introductions these nice and friendly people drove us down to a small village of very old, English looking buildings on the river. As the tallest building in the village, Saskatchewan University stood out prominently. We were taken to Dr. Haslam's house, where we were given a room of our own. "No need to pay," they insisted. We were stunned with such hospitality. We had money, $100, and could have paid, but they refused to accept anything.

Dr. Haslam's wife insisted we live with them the first weeks and have our meals with them. There would be so much to get used to. Their next-door neighbors, an older gentleman called Mr. Woodley and his daughter, May, were quite interested in us and wanted to help. They had us over for dinner often and were very eager to hear about this little country Norway that we had left. We had our first Thanksgiving dinner at their house, and old Mr. Woodley taught me how to cook the turkey, stuffing and all (and to this day I prepare my turkey Mr. Woodley's way). I had never seen a turkey in my life before, dead or alive; it was an enormous bird. In Norway we never had turkey. Sometimes we would have chickens, but they were small and used mostly for soup.

After some weeks, Mr. Woodley found an apartment for us on the third floor of a friend's house. It had high windows from which the summer breeze would cool us off and the winter storms make us shiver in our beds. But we enjoyed having a home of our own, with the chair from the garbage dump and the little table Mr. Woodley had let us borrow, and we were very glad the apartment came with a big double bed.

The first time I cooked a chicken, I had a talk with the butcher. "Use lots of water in the pot and let it boil until the legs feel loose," he said. I followed his instructions and watched our first chicken cook. When the water turned green, I knew something was wrong. What could be wrong? When Jan Per came home we inspected the bird in that yellow green soup, and he found I had cooked the chicken with all the intestines still inside! But how was I to know that in Canada they sell chickens with all its intestines inside? The chicken was expensive, and we were poor, so we cleaned the bird off and cooked it a little longer in fresh clean water before we sat down to dinner. It tasted great. Next time I met the butcher he asked how the "Scandihuvians" dinner had been. When I told him, he went into a hysterical laughing spell!

Months later we got a better apartment, and it was here we experienced our coldest winter, -29° in the daytime. But the Canadians sent their kids outside to play, so I did too. We had two boys now, and the oldest went outside bundled up so only his eyes showed. Still he got frostbite on his cheek—a big white spot that took many months before it disappeared.

One day I received an invitation to a tea at Mrs. Currie's house, the wife of Professor Currie who was the dean of the physics department. It was going to be a serious affair, people told me, a real English tea party. We had to dress up and even wear hats and gloves. I was glad I was forewarned and spent days looking for a hat, dragging my little kids around from store to store until I found it….an elegant white feather hat.

Mrs. Currie would be pouring; she sat at the end of the table in a beautiful pink silk dress and hat and made an effort to converse with all the newcomers. I was suddenly asked to tell a little about Norway. "Did people have cars? Refrigerators? What about televisions? What do you eat?" I explained as well as I could, in my poor English, how we lived. No one had TVs, not many owned a car, we used busses and trains, and refrigerators were not necessary. When it came to what kind of food we ate, it was easy…mostly fish. "What about ham and beef?" they asked. "Well," I said, "that is very expensive, but we often have sheep meat and garbage." Mrs. Currie smiled sweetly as she looked up from her pouring, "Maybe you mean lamb and cabbage?" I realized my mistake right away, but the ladies had a hard time trying not to laugh. The little feather hats were shaking all around me. "Yes, lamb and cabbage," I stammered with a red face. When I arrived home Jan Per had to hear about my tea. My son, Knut, then five years old, will never forget it. He thought it was hilarious. "In Norway they eat sheep meat and garbage!" Of course he had to tell everyone, and it became a family joke.

We had been in Canada three years when we learned that Jan Per's thesis would not be accepted. His earlier degree from the University of Oslo had, of course, been written in Norwegian, and they had no way of determining if it was acceptable. He had to take another year to do all his Norwegian exams over again in English. It was very disappointing. So we stayed on and endured another cold winter with snow storms and below freezing temperatures. Summer brought sandstorms, with sand even invading our refrigerator. But we got a car—an old Austin with a large, gaping hole in the floor. We bought a piece of linoleum and covered it up, and our car floor now had beautiful big red roses that would cheer up anybody who stepped inside.

I was very big and uncomfortably pregnant with our third son, Paul, when Jan Per needed me to help with his thesis. His papers, at last, were all in order and he was now ready to get his Ph.D. The baby was also ready to come any time, but it must have sensed that it had to wait until this ceremony was over. It was a wonderful day when Jan Per finally got his diploma, his Ph.D. from the University of Saskatchewan. Now the future was ours.

Arriving home from the ceremony, we had left two-year old Per downstairs alone for a few minutes while we changed our clothing upstairs. The diploma with the golden seal and the beautiful red silk ribbon was left on the table, unfortunately next to a little pair of nail scissors. When we came downstairs, we found little Per sitting on the floor in a heap of paper clippings; he had cut the diploma to pieces. I took my son away in a hurry. I was afraid of how Jan Per would react, but I will never forget how well he managed the situation after the initial shock. I had always loved him, but now I had to admire him. Later on he got another diploma, but never one with the golden seal.

With his credentials earned, Jan Per got a job in New York City, so we packed our belongings and said good-bye to our Canadian friends. We were just about ready to leave when we realized little Per had disappeared. After a frantic search with all the neighbors, he was finally found blocks away. When we all five finally sat down on the train headed to New York, I with the baby in my arms, life seemed great. That the baby happened to get sick and let it spill all over the jacket I had just got from Norway did not really matter too much, maybe except for the lingering smell.

We rented a little house on Long Island. It had a dirty dining room floor, dirty carpet in the living room, and a very dirty, old-fashioned kitchen where you could scrape the old fat off the walls. I spent many hours cleaning this house, with three small guys crawling and playing around me. For three years we lived here while Jan Per worked for St. John's University He got a better car as he tried to get used to the New York traffic, but for more than half a year he did not have time to get a driver's license. After his first fender bender when a policeman showed up, he finally got scared enough to get his license.

I never liked living in New York. With small children it was difficult to enjoy what the city had to offer, and long rides, traffic jams, and crying children made getting to the parks and the beaches outside of the city a challenge. I was homesick and miserable. Jan Per promised he would try to find another job and a better place to live, and I took our three boys home to Norway for an extended visit with my parents. When I returned to the States six months later, this time on a fancy airline, Jan Per had found some new job possibilities. One was in Monterey, California, the other in Buffalo, New York. He was quite excited. "Buffalo has snow in the winter so we could ski, and the University has a reactor with possibilities for research, and it is also closer to Norway," he said. But I had heard about the Mafia in Buffalo and was worried.

It was August of 1962 when we drove to Buffalo, and when I saw the University on the hill with all the old elm trees clustered around it, I felt I could be happy here. So we settled down, had two more kids, a boy and finally a daughter. After a few years we bought a little house. The first years were difficult. The reactor was too small, not possible to use for much research, but his colleagues were friendly and nice so he liked his teaching job. We did have snow and the kids learned to ski, and we became familiar with and enjoyed all the big parks around the city, which became a lifesaver for me. Every Sunday we were out somewhere exploring, hiking, skiing, or swimming. It was not like Norway where we were ten to fifteen minutes away from the ocean or the mountains, but it helped. We found many friends at the University, and I became involved with the International Women's Club.

Then suddenly in 1971 Jan Per heard of a job opening in Norway at Trondheim University. We had been in Sweden on a sabbatical leave the year before and decided we should finally go back for good. We had never been in Trondheim before, but the pay was right and it sounded great. The University in Norway offered to pay for the trip across the ocean, so we took everything with us—all the Swedish furniture we had bought the year before on our sabbatical as well as the piano, after finding someone to make a big box to transport it in. Tears were shed as we said good-bye to our friends. We had been living in North America for seventeen years. Jan Per had not been home in all these years, but I had visited twice. Our oldest son was seventeen and ready for college soon, and our daughter, the youngest, was five. It was very exciting; we had wanted it so badly to happen for such a long time.

At first it was wonderful to be back. The apartment was modern and roomy in a big apartment building with a fancy playground for the kids and just steps from the forest and a little lake—great for swimming and hiking and long skiing trips in the winter. I loved it. The schools were good, our kids were happy and busy with lots of after school activities—chess club, canoe club, ski trips, gymnastics etc. I was busy setting food on the table every night. I had no car but could take the bus downtown to shop for food. It seemed like we ate so much more in Norway than in the U.S. The kids were always hungry. Maybe it was the fish diet. Meat was too expensive; it was for holidays only.

But Jan Per found his job disappointing. He was less independent in his work, and the promised research never happened. There just was no money available. Norway was still struggling to rebuild. We learned that the house we had hoped for would not be available for two more years, and we could not get our own phone until the next year. While the kids were happy, everything seemed so difficult. I saved money by learning to bake bread, cook all sorts of fish dinners, butcher pig and sheep carcasses, and buy food in bulk that could be stored in a cold basement. I found it hard to get acquainted with the Norwegians in Trondheim. Since Jan Per and I were both from southern Norway, our dialect was different, as well as our culture. We simply did not fit in.

When a letter came from America, it took us by surprise. "Are you staying there or coming back in the fall? Please let us know." Jan Per had been granted a leave of absence from the University in Buffalo, and we had thought we would be able to stay for two years to get used to this new life in our old country. But we had to decide now after just one year. Jan Per was not happy at work. I was not happy living in the apartment without a phone and being far down on a waiting list to get a house. We heard we might get a chance in a couple of years...maybe. We had to face the fact: Norway was not an easy country to live in with five hungry children.

Our children with my mother and her friend before we left Norway

We decided to go back. Our family could not understand...had we lost our minds? But Jan Per would be happy, so once again the packing started. The old piano box was found in the basement and could serve us again. In July, Jan Per and I went back and found a house in Clarence, NY, not far from the University of Buffalo, where we still live today. Back in Norway we rented a big container for all our furniture and household belongings and had it sent back to the States. This time the bill had to be paid by us.

It was difficult to leave, and I cried when the plane took off. The kids were also very sorry. My mother was sorry we were leaving but understood and said she would come to visit us soon. On the way back, as I sat on the plane, I was fighting with my emotions. I had loved this country so much, it was hard to leave, but my husband was happy, and was that not what really mattered? Knowing I had mixed emotions, Jan Per promised me that we would go back on vacations—we did not have to cut Norway out completely.

Some difficult years followed, but we eventually settled down. The U.S. was now our home. We finally got rid of our green cards—our permanent residency cards—and took our oaths of citizenship. We even learned to sing some of the national hymns that we now sing as a group at the senior center during exercise classes.

The University of Buffalo treated us well. We have had a good life here, and today our children are well-educated Americans. The year in Norway, however, was an eye-opener for them. They experienced a different way of life and hopefully learned something from it. Did we do the right thing moving back and forth across the ocean? I do not know. We, like all parents, always did what we thought was right at the time, what was best for the family. Our children and even our grandchildren have been back visiting our old country. They have learned about Norway, they know their roots, they are proud of their family and ancestry.

Do we miss Norway? Not so much anymore. But in Norway we missed many things about the U.S. The people are friendly in Norway but set in their ways. I missed the American openness, the sense of humor and flexibility. After we bought a cabin in the Adirondacks we felt closer to the real America. I have seen much of the wonderful country we are now lucky to live in as we traveled throughout the U.S., and I have realized that Norway is not the only country that is beautiful. This world has lots of beauty to offer us on any continent—you just have to look for it.

At a UB Physics Department function in 1972

From Radars to Airplanes

Bill Scott

I grew up in Shinglehouse, a small borough in the northwest corner of Pennsylvania about ninety miles south of Buffalo. The oldest of seven, I was born at home in 1931; the rest of my siblings were born at the nearby hospital. With a population around 1200, life in Shinglehouse was pretty simple. As a teenager I worked in the gas fields owned by my uncle, earning seventy-five cents an hour, and I also occupied myself raising Beagles. One day in 1950, after I had graduated from high school, I was out working in the dog pen when my brother and a couple friends came up and said, "Hey, Bill, we're going to join the Air Force...want to come?" "Sure," I replied, setting down my shovel, and off we went, hitchhiking to Olean. When we got to Olean my brother changed his mind, but I signed up.

I spent four years in the Air Force and gained valuable experience that would eventually be useful in my career. At Griffiss Air Force Base in Rome, NY I attended Radar School for one year, and I then spent seven months installing height finder radars along the coastline of Japan. Fifty foot towers were first installed, then radars that could detect the height of airplanes flying overhead were mounted on top of the towers. It was a great assignment that I enjoyed very much.

A height finder radar tower

1952

After being discharged from the Air Force I attended Penn State, graduating in 1958 with a degree in Electrical Engineering. Shortly thereafter I was hired at Sylvania Electric. On my first day I noticed a young secretary named Jane and decided right then and there that I was going to marry her, and eventually I did. While working at Sylvania for the next decade, I attended night classes at the University of Buffalo, earning a Master's Degree in Business. I was then hired at Sierra Research in 1967, where I worked for the next twenty-six years.

I was involved in many projects over the years at Sierra, working on government contracts in electronics and radar. My first assignment was working with the FAA (Federal Aviation Administration) to design a collision avoidance system that would be used in civilian airplanes. At the time I was hired there were ninety-seven employees, but as we gained government contracts, more and more people were hired, eventually growing to over thirteen hundred. In between the government work we did research on and manufactured everything from rain-making systems to rat-repellant sonar devices. One of our biggest contracts came in the early 1980s and involved updating missile detecting radar systems in U.S. Army box vans. The vehicles had been warehoused for decades and were being updated to be used in Europe to detect and intercept Russian missiles, which was a major concern at the time. The back of these vehicles were jammed with outdated electronics, and we updated all the components in about one hundred and twenty-five of them. The project took several years and was followed by my biggest and final assignment at Sierra.

The Norwegian government wanted to add F-16 fighter jets to their fleet, which cost millions and millions of dollars each. But an F-5 jet, made in the early fifties, could be retrofitted for about a million dollars to have the same appearance and performance as an F-16. We were awarded the contract to do the conversions, and I was selected to meet with the Norwegian Air Force to design the planes. I travelled to

Norway several times over the course of the project, staying about two weeks each time. I also went to England a couple times to meet with a sub-contractor, which worked out well for me because, by this time, my three children were grown and my son was stationed in England working for the National Security Agency. Jane went with me on these trips, and we stayed for a month each time to visit our son.

Norway had acquired the F-5s from the U.S. government, and Norwegian pilots flew the planes to Buffalo. Once we received each plane, it was totally dismantled and then reassembled as we upgraded the avionics. All the electrical components were replaced, which included everything from the throttles and instrument panels to the communications and navigations systems. There were hundreds of controls and systems on each plane that were modernized, and afterward a pilot sitting in the cockpit could not tell the difference between the converted F-5 and a modern F-16. To test the capabilities of the refurbished planes, the Norwegian pilots would engage in mock "dogfights" with American pilots flying F-16s at the Niagara Falls Air Base, and the performance of the two planes was equal.

Over the course of eight years, we converted seven single pilot planes and eight double pilot planes, spending about six months and hundreds of hours on each plane. The project was completed in 1993, and I then retired from Sierra after a long and most interesting career.

One of our converted F-5 airplanes flies over Niagara Falls, NY

The Dancer

Michael Valentic

Modern society has often placed a stigma on young boys and men who happen to enjoy activities traditionally dominated by females. While girls and women who join in male-dominated activities are generally seen as strong and confident, the same does not usually hold true for us men. Are boys and men who participate in dance any less masculine than those who participate in, let's say, football or wresting? As I have been blessed with a lifetime of enjoyment and success in all these activities, I can say with certainty that this stigma is not justified.

My mother enrolled me in my first dance class when I was six years old. We lived in the small town of Turtle Creek, Pennsylvania, just outside of Pittsburgh. Mother had wanted at one time to be a dancer but never had the opportunity, so she hoped, as many parents do, to pass that unfulfilled desire on to me. At first I danced just to please her, but I soon developed my own love for both tap and jazz. I excelled immediately, and by the time I was eight years old I was chosen to appear on the locally televised "Wilkins Talent Show." Shortly thereafter, in

1947, my dad's job at Westinghouse relocated us to Buffalo, where I continued my training at the Geraldine Hoffman School of Dance in Cheektowaga. Under Geraldine's expert instruction, my dancing skills flourished, and I added ballet to my repertoire.

As a youngster I had often been teased, and occasionally beat up, for being "the dancer." I guess today we would say I'd been bullied. But once I reached high school, my dancing skills became quite an asset—it was a lot easier to meet girls when you could dance with them! While at Maryvale High School I also ran track and played tennis, each for one year, and I played football and participated in wrestling for three years each. Wrestling was, in fact, the sport in which I excelled. I was team captain and high scorer from 1954-1956, and I was first-runner up in sectionals in my senior year.

In spite of my involvement in sports, dancing continued to be a priority. I was selected to participate in "Mrs. Dunn's Stars of Tomorrow," a premiere dance group that performed at area clubs and local events and appeared several times on local television. My schedule was busy, to say the least, but little did I know that all my extra-curricular activities were preparing me for an exciting career.

At seventeen I enlisted in the U.S. Army Reserves. I had received a wrestling scholarship to attend Waynesburg College (now a University) in Waynesburg, Pennsylvania, fifty miles south of Pittsburgh. The college had just instituted a mutual program with the Army to allow students to participate in the Reserves while simultaneously enrolled in college classes. As I earned a degree in Physical Education, I also gained valuable experience through my military service and training, spending time at both Camp Drum in New York and Fort Dix in New Jersey. I spent a total of six years in the Army Reserves, the last two as a chaplain's assistant, an assignment that may have been influenced by my early years as an altar server at church.

Appearing on the WBEN Talent Show

After completing both my undergraduate degree and my term in the reserves, I enrolled at the University of Buffalo to pursue my master's degree. At UB I once again captained the wrestling team for three years, and in my final year of college I also had the opportunity to serve as a trainer for the "All America Game" that was being played at the old War Memorial Stadium in Buffalo. This football game featured the top college players in the country, East against West, several of whom went on to become NFL Hall of Famers.

Upon graduating from UB with a master's degree, I was offered a job as a physical education teacher at the Maryvale elementary school, a position I held from 1962 until 1995. During my teaching career, I also co-coached varsity football from 1963 to 1965, including Maryvale's first ever championship football team in 1964. But just as in high school and college, I found even more success with wrestling. From 1967 through 1970, I coached the wrestling team, and each of those four years I had at least one sectional champion and one wrestler in the top four in the New York State championship. One of my wrestlers was even featured in Sports Illustrated. But my proudest moment was preparing two wrestlers to compete at the 1968 World Competition held in Rome, Italy, both of whom went on to win silver medals.

Throughout these years of playing and coaching sports, dancing remained my first love. In 1961 I opened my own dance studio, The Performing Arts Center, while continuing to teach and coach at Maryvale. My days were long and hectic, but I was doing things that I loved. I would teach all day, go home and grab a bite to eat, then head to the dance studio or out to a sporting event. I thoroughly enjoyed teaching and training youngsters to develop their skills in whatever sport they chose to participate, be it wrestling, football, or dancing. I had married and eventually had five children, and it was only natural that they all became immersed in the world of dance, each to varying degrees. One of my daughters was offered a job as a dancer in Las Vegas; the others eventually pursued other interests, and I am so very proud of all of them.

Because I was involved in coaching athletes, I began to realize that there was no competitive field for dancing. I knew firsthand that dancers worked and trained as hard as any other athlete, but other than the yearly recital attended by family and friends, they received little recognition for their accomplishments. I thought there should be something for dancers to strive for, a goal that would encourage them to reach their greatest potential in their sport. And so was born the idea for "Summerdanse."

Modeled after gymnastics and ice skating competitions, I organized the first regional dance competition, held at Studio Arena Theater in 1970. Participants came from all over New York State, as well as from Ohio, Pennsylvania, New Jersey, and Canada, to compete both as groups and in solo competition in tap, jazz, ballet, and acrobatics. There were a couple glitches the first year. We greatly underestimated the length of the competition—we had expected it to last several hours, but it was 2:00 in the morning when the dancers had all competed and awards were handed out by the judges. But no one seemed to mind and it turned out to be a wonderful and memorable event.

Plans began immediately afterward to continue and expand the competition. Summerdanse—purposely spelled to generate questions—flourished and in time was held in cities throughout New York, Ohio, Pennsylvania, and Canada. Each year thousands of dancers, including plenty of boys, enthusiastically participated in what grew to be two, three and four day competitions held in schools, hotels, and convention centers. Prize money was generated through entrance fees, sponsors, and fundraisers held by dedicated parents and grew from the original $3 for solo winners and $1.50 for group participants to $25 for solos and $10 for groups. But the competition was not solely about winning and prizes. It was meant to be educational and to build self-confidence, and every dancer was recognized for their efforts. Fun and friendship were always part of the events, and some of the proceeds were donated to various charities.

My wife Audrey and I continued to organize and produce Summerdanse, traveling to each competition, until 1995, when I also retired from teaching at both my Performing Arts Dance Studio and the Maryvale schools. We turned the leadership over to one of our capable associates, and the competition continues today with participants ranging in age from six to adult. It has expanded to include modern dance, musical theater, and hip hop. Following the success of Summerdanse, many other dance competitions sprung up around the country, precursors to the wildly popular television shows "Dancing with the Stars," and "So You Think You Can Dance."

My football and wrestling days ended long ago, but I continue to embrace my love of teaching and dance at area senior centers. And although I was often teased as a dancer over the years, and just as often praised for my accomplishments in football and wrestling, I can say with pride that it was a mingling of many years of involvement in all three activities that contributed to my happiness and satisfaction in life. I ask again, does my life as a dancer make me any less masculine? I would say not. Dancing is liberating, motivating, relaxing, and challenging. So if any young boys—or any senior men—have any desire to take up dancing, to you I say, "Kick up your heels and go for it!"

What Whitey Did

Ruth Weaver

"Uh oh...what did Whitey do now?" We must have uttered those words a hundred times over the years. Whenever an unrecognized car pulled into the driveway or an unfamiliar face came to the door (often with Whitey in tow), this was always our first thought. And rightfully so. You see, Whitey, an English bulldog, had a tendency to wander around town and make himself at home wherever he went.

Whitey came to us just as the Great Depression was winding down. It was 1940, when I was eleven years old, and we were living in Niagara Falls, NY. Sadly, we'd had to have our first beloved English bulldog named Tuggy euthanized several months before. My parents had bought Tuggy as soon as they were married and wanted nothing but another English bulldog. So they went back to the same breeder who had sold them Tuggy, but he'd said he wouldn't have a puppy available for about six months. Mom and Dad told him they'd wait, but just a few weeks later, the breeder called.

A friend of his who was also a breeder had gone to check on an English bulldog that she had recently sold. It was a hot summer day, so she was shocked to find the dog, who was almost a year old, tethered outside on a short chain with no shade or water to be seen. She stopped by again the next day, only to find the same scenario. So, as the people had not yet fully paid for the young dog, she went up to the porch, unchained him, and took him home, leaving a note that she took the dog back because it was not being cared for properly. Then she let her breeder friend know that she had an English bulldog available for adoption.

And that's how we got Whitey. Even though my younger sister and I had wanted a puppy, we quickly fell in love with him. It took some coaxing for Whitey to trust us; he had obviously been mistreated, and he was just as obviously afraid of chains. So Dad bought a leather leash for him, and with lots of love and attention, Whitey gradually adjusted to us and to his new home. He loved to be outside and run around the yard, and he even took a liking to our black cat. But as I said, the Depression had just ended, and just a few months after we got Whitey, we had to move so my dad could find work.

Dad's uncle had a hardware store in Herkimer, NY and offered him a job, which my dad eagerly accepted. So we packed up our belongings, said good-bye to the neighbors, and headed across the state. Herkimer was a nice little village located in Central New York in the foothills of the Adirondack Mountains, halfway between Syracuse and Albany. It was much smaller than Niagara Falls and housing was not as readily available. Fortunately Dad's uncle also owned a four-family apartment building, and we were able to rent one of these units. The only drawback was that the yard was not fenced in. As Mom had also taken a part-time job, and my sister and I were in school, none of us would be home during the day. But Whitey was now an active, outgoing, two-year old dog who, typical to his breed, demanded lots of human interaction. It would have been almost cruel, at least from his point of view, to keep him cooped up in the upper apartment all day while we were gone. As he was still very much afraid of being chained, that was not an option, and he would have chewed right through the leather leash. So on the days she worked, Mom had no choice but to leave him in the backyard when she left. Well Whitey, left to his own devices, decided to make the most of this newfound freedom!

With Whitey, Mother & my sister

It didn't take long for folks to learn that this friendly dog trotting around town on his short legs was named Whitey. Like all bulldogs, with his oversized head and stout body, Whitey could look intimidating. But he soon became known as a gentle, affectionate dog, and people seemed to take his presence for granted. Most of the time. Word got around that Whitey belonged to Mr. Weaver at the hardware store, and folks would stop in and tell my dad, "Whitey is over at the bakery." "Just saw Whitey at the church." "I bought Whitey some lunch at the diner." My uncle even kept a spittoon full of water for him, and Whitey would stop in for a drink when he was thirsty. As time went on, Whitey became both more well-known and more adventurous. Traffic would stop to let him cross the street. All the police officers knew him. And the local grocer would sometimes throw him a ham bone, which Whitey would relish and drag home.

Before we had moved to Herkimer, while still living in Niagara Falls, we often played games of touch football with the neighborhood kids. Whitey naturally joined right in, always trying to get the ball. Unfortunately he didn't realize when he saw the Herkimer high school football games being played on a field near our new home that his participation would not be as welcome. One day the coach came to our house, schedule in hand, and asked us to please keep Whitey in on the days they had a game. But Whitey did become known at the high school, located across the street from our house, and sometimes sat outside the door. So it apparently didn't faze him, one day, to trot right in when someone opened the door. "Whitey was in the school today," was the report we later heard.

As he grew, and as he became more familiar with the town, Whitey spent more and more time outside, often not coming home until evening. He was a good-sized dog, weighing about forty pounds, so he wasn't too content to be confined to a small apartment when he could be exploring a whole town. Usually Whitey was happy to wander around and visit, stopping to rest when he needed to. But if he had an opportunity to investigate someplace new, he usually jumped right in. Just like at the school, Whitey sometimes sat outside the door of any one of the local churches. And sure enough, an aggravated minister one day stopped at the house to let us know that Whitey, having once again taken advantage of an open door, had joined in the procession that morning. An usher had quickly got hold of him and ushered him right out the door, but the minister was not too happy about Whitey's irreverent intrusion. After the church escapade, we started keeping better tabs on Whitey on Sunday mornings.

Although Herkimer in the early 1940s was a small, working class town, there was an area of stately, Victorian homes where the wealthy people lived. One day, as my parents happened to drive by these lovely homes, Mother spotted Whitey relaxing in a big wicker chair on a wide front porch. Not daring to stop, they drove on home; Whitey, as usual, wandered home later that afternoon. A couple days later, Mother heard a car pull up

104

in front of the house and looked out to see a luxurious, black sedan parked in the street. A uniformed chauffeur stepped out, walked around to the passenger side, and opened the door. Out jumped Whitey as naturally as if it was his own car. The driver told Mother that the woman he worked for enjoyed Whitey and liked to have him visit. Fortunately Whitey wore tags, so they, like many people in town, could see where Whitey lived and were able to bring him home. This scenario was repeated several more times as Whitey continued rubbing elbows with the upper class.

Our socially skilled dog was not limited to mingling with adults. One day we looked out the window to see two little girls, who we didn't even know, strolling down the street pushing Whitey in an oversized doll carriage! Someone had obviously picked him up and put him in the carriage, because he could not have jumped that high on his own and the young girls certainly could not have lifted him. But he seemed to be thoroughly enjoying both the ride and the attention.

Whitey enjoying his buggy ride

We later learned that the girls' father, an inspector at a lumber camp in the nearby Adirondack Mountains, had indeed put Whitey in the buggy. He also told us that Whitey had several times accompanied him on inspections, riding along in the front seat of his car, and that he'd bought Whitey lunch at the lumber camp. The inspector and his daughters had become so fond of Whitey that he offered my dad $1000 for him, quite a large amount of money at that time. Of course my father refused the offer—there was no way we could part with Whitey!

We lived in Herkimer for four or five years then moved to Kenmore, just outside Buffalo. Whitey, and all of us, learned quickly that his days of carefree roaming had come to an end. At first he stayed close to our new home when he was let out, but one day he was gone much too long. My dad started calling around and found out that Whitey had been picked up and taken to the dog pound in Buffalo, and he promptly drove over and rescued him. Fortunately Mother wasn't working as much then and could keep an eye on Whitey's wanderings. He still managed to get out and explore from time to time, but now that the dog warden knew him he was never picked up again.

Whitey only lived to be about seven years old, but even after he was gone people still asked about him. He left us and many others with a wealth of happy memories, and thinking about his many adventures still makes me smile and chuckle. Because, after all, that's what Whitey did!

Surprise!

Clare Crowley

When I was eight years old, my mom was pregnant. In those days, kids knew nothing—and I mean NOTHING—about "the birds and the bees." It was a hush-hush topic, so I was unsure of what was to happen. At the time, 1936, the family consisted of four children: an older brother, my twin brother and me, and a younger brother.

It was after supper on an October evening when Dad told us older ones to go upstairs to the bedroom and "stay there." That was unusual, since only the boys slept up there, so I guess I was thrilled to share the evening with them. Our three year old brother stayed downstairs because he was already asleep and would remain so through the coming event anyway.

The bathroom was downstairs, so when I awoke the next morning, down the stairs I went. I opened the door which led to the kitchen, and lo and behold, I saw a crib and my dad standing next to it. I went over to the crib and looked in, and there was a baby at one end and another at the other end. What a surprise! A girl baby and a boy baby—twins! I was so excited that I ran upstairs to tell my brothers about the blessed event I had discovered, even though I did not know where they had come from. When I went to school that morning, I told my third grade teacher, as she always set aside time for news before starting our lessons. You can be sure my story was noted on the blackboard!

As time passed, there were eventually seven children in our family. Paul, now 88, who is two years older than me and my twin Leon, who died in 1985; Bill, 81, Bob, 78 (his twin of that memorable night, Roberta, died in 1994); and Jerry, 73. God truly blessed us with wonderful parents who were examples of living faith and unending love.

Mother with twins Bob and Roberta

A Tribute to Mom

Sandi Kintzel

Each year on Mother's Day I fondly recall and pay homage to "The World's Greatest Mom." I know that's what she was because her coffee cup said so, and you just don't give a cup like that to a mediocre mom! She cherished that cup from the moment her three small daughters pooled their pennies to get it for her one Mother's Day many years ago.

Mom was widowed at an early age with three small girls to raise on her own, and although it was extremely hard, she did a darn good job of it. Putting us first was always her top priority. We never knew we were poor because there was an abundance of love in our home. Mom showed us that material things were not important and that love for each other was. On Christmas, we were satisfied and thrilled with just one gift, usually an article of clothing—sometimes new and sometimes purchased from a consignment shop. I guess my penchant for visiting thrift stores and consignment shops now is a throwback to my youth and upbringing. Even today I am frugal when it comes to throwing things out; I'm always looking for a way to give an article a second life as something else! I still remember Mom using the wax liner from a cereal box as wax paper to wrap up a sandwich for lunch or using a plastic bread bag to keep something fresh in the refrigerator...or to keep our feet dry from a leaky boot! The love notes she left us were usually written on utility bill envelopes. We never owned a car so taking a bus was our only means of transportation. How often she would walk miles to and from an appointment so that she could give us girls ten cents apiece to go to a Saturday movie.

The word love was used many times a day in our home, and expressions of love were just as frequent. Each night before going to bed and whenever we left the house were always accompanied by a kiss. To this day, my children—two boys—and grandchildren give my husband and me an "I love you" along with their goodbye kiss, another throwback to my mother and her expression of love for me and my sisters.

I could go on and on citing her attributes. Mom has been gone almost forty years, but she left behind a legacy of how to love and to give of yourself unselfishly. I only hope that when I am gone, my family remembers my love for them and feels the same way about me. If there is someone you love, don't be afraid to tell them. They will remember it and love you for it. I LOVE YOU MOM!!

With Mother before my friend's wedding

A Degree of Satisfaction

Violet Oldenski

In the 1980s, three of my daughters were already in college, and I was beginning to feel that I was losing them physically as well as intellectually. Since I had married right out of high school, I hadn't had the opportunity to pursue my education. You raise six kids on a limited budget and you let your dreams slide. As my kids were getting to the point of independence, I felt that this was my time also.

Unfortunately, being "old school," my husband didn't share my views, and I had to make my own money for tuition, which I did by babysitting, couponing, and rebating. At the time two competing stores were doing triple coupons in South Rochester, and with the aid of their ads, my coupons, and rebates, I saved quite a bit from my shopping budget, often spending just $10 or $20 on a $200 order. We lived in Royalton, a rural town in the southeast corner of Niagara County, so between shopping and hauling the kids around, my old station wagon sure earned its keep. I was determined that my kids would not miss out on anything having to do with education, be it 4-H, Scouts, sports, extracurricular, or social events, so being a chauffeur was a major part of my life. After spending the summer teaching myself Algebra so I could pass the Math requirements, I enrolled in Niagara County Community College (NCCC) under an Associate Degree.

I began my long overdue voyage of self-discovery in a stark classroom surrounded by excited, noisy students who were on a voyage of their own. More apprehensive than excited, I wondered how I would fit in...a forty year old who was probably the age of most of the students' mothers. Then I realized I didn't have to fit in because I was free from oppression and other peoples' expectations. My rite of passage had been fulfilled a long time ago and I still had my dreams.

My first class was in journalism under a stuffy stereotypical professor in a three-piece suit and tight tie. I was mesmerized by his tie. It threatened to choke him as he moved his fleshy jowls this way and that, and I wondered why men subjected themselves to that. I sat in the back corner so I could unobtrusively scan the room. It was harder for my classmates to stare at me there—the odd man out. The women usually clustered together and had their private conversations while the young men engaged in the age-old ritual of boasting and appraisal. As they furtively checked each other out, it seemed that many of the students thought that finding a mate was *the* major college course.

Another class was in Creative Writing with a professor who recognized the hunger to learn that was within me. I remember the first day I entered his class. He strode decisively into the classroom, and his leather boots and open necked flannel shirt were certainly unexpected. His hair was thick and black and continued down into a wooly full beard. Unruly eyebrows cloaked dark unfathomable eyes. He dropped his books on the desk with a thud and announced his name. He stated that if we weren't prepared to work, we were in the wrong room. The voice of authority had arrived! With eyes void of emotion, he scoped the classroom. When his eyes held mine for a moment, I wanted to run from the room, but his eyes commanded me not to. He gave me a barely perceptible smile and a slight nod as if acknowledging that I had come to the right room and was welcome. Over the months, that classroom became a haven for me in an otherwise unfriendly atmosphere. The other students ignored me as they walked hand in hand in the hallway or conversed in small intimate groups. They were secure in the knowledge that they fit in. They were with their own kind, fulfilling expectations and striving for the same desired goals. I searched for a sense of self.

It had been twenty-five years since I attempted any writing, and the mechanics were difficult for me. The rules of punctuation came back slowly. I learned that the professor's eyes were not unfathomable, but rather kind and gentle; you could give up your soul to them and it would be safe and nourished. Without reservations, I revealed my innermost thoughts, pain, and frustrations, and he plowed through it all. The patience he must have had to read through all those pages of heartache. With his gentle prodding and unconditional understanding, ideas I had never been allowed to express began to flow. He understood that it had been a long time since I had attempted any writing and patiently explained the grammatical errors but never counted them against me. Now the content was another matter. "You're good at the celebration of life," he told me, "but you're better than that!" That statement has been my mantra ever since. He always pushed and expected more, and I still try to see the good in everything, but I now push to see more—to be empathetic. I have to admit that much of my writing was full of frustration, and he became my therapist as well as my instructor. I learned that writing was my coping skill, and I will always be grateful to him for that.

My English classes helped me get through those difficult years. I was still a mother and wife—a homemaker—and often stayed up nights to finish assignments. Some days, days when I dreaded entering that school with all those bright, cheerful, students, so full of life and expectations, my writing classes drew me back. I didn't have the friendships and support systems that most of the students had; I was all prim and polyester to their jeans and t-shirts, but I had the hunger and that was enough to keep me going. The quiet, isolated library became my second home until I graduated with high honors.

In the early 1990s, shortly after my husband died, I enrolled in classes at the University of Buffalo. One of my daughters said I was foolish, that I should just get a job instead of paying all that money for an education. She didn't realize that my need wasn't about money; it was about coping and finding the real me—not a wife, nor mother, but a self-actualized woman. I started in the Social Science Interdisciplinary, Gerontology program. Since the last year had been spent taking care of my husband, I felt that was the way to go. I soon found it was too depressing, so I switched to Early Childhood, with a minor in English. Again, the writing classes kept me going. At that time, I was dating a man who fully supported everything I was attempting. I no longer hid in the school library; I came home to a wonderful meal made by a loving companion. He knew my studies were primary and even audited a few classes with me. Having a support system and my English classes carried my through. I completed all of my requirements, except for one class in my English minor, when I received a job offer I couldn't refuse.

When I retired in 2000, I moved to Clarence and became heavily involved in the Senior Center. In 2010, now 70, I decided to finish my final English requirement at UB and received my Bachelor Degree, cum laude. Education has given me confidence and a greater scope to my life than I ever expected.

But that's not the end. In 2012 I went to ECC for Poetry. Again, I lucked out with my professor. He was supportive, but also a "no nonsense" kind of instructor who demanded participation. I no longer hid in the back of the class. Since I was a few years older than him, we were comfortable with each other and interacted in a comfortable, open teacher/student relationship. I considered him a friend. Instead of feeling like an inferior intruder among the students,

I now felt as if I belonged and I could contribute and interact with the students. My professor told me he was considering adding an advanced class the next semester and asked if I would consider joining them. Well, yes! That was like asking if I wanted a second piece of chocolate. Some things are just too good to pass up. I was chosen to read some of my work several times, and by the end of that second semester I was able to speak publicly—something I could never do before.

So what is it like being a "nontraditional" student? For me, initially, it was frightening, exhausting, and lonely. The second time around, it was exhilarating. Life seemed fuller, and I felt young again, as if anything was possible. The third time around was _fun_. I entered a new phase of my life which allowed me to be confident and fulfilled.

Don't count me out yet. There is still much to learn...

The Reunion

Martha Wicksell

At some point along the way, parents often have to love their children enough to let them go—to their first day of school, their first sleepover, summer camp, college—the separation can be difficult for both, but it is part of growing up. Sadly, I had to let go of my daughter before I ever got to hold on.

In 1958 after graduating from Erie County Technical Institute in Buffalo, I found a job with Stouffer's Restaurant, which was based in Cleveland. At nineteen years old I would be traveling from city to city as the Pantry Supervisor for newly opened restaurants. My parents drove me to Cleveland, and I still remember my mother crying and crying as they dropped me off at the house I would be staying in. I was the oldest of her four children and the first one to leave home. Looking back on that moment is a bittersweet memory.

For over five years I traveled around the country, opening stores in Chicago, Philadelphia, and Detroit. I would stay in each city for about a year which made it difficult to maintain a relationship. But in Detroit I met a man and thought we were in love, and in early spring of 1962 I found out I was pregnant. Shortly thereafter I drove to New York City to pick up my parents from the airport after their trip to Germany then drove them home to Buffalo. Before I had a chance to tell them I was pregnant, my mother, with the keen eye that mothers have, noticed the bump in my belly. I wish I could say that my parents offered me their support, but unfortunately that was not the case. As an unwed mother-to-be, my parents disowned me. And when the baby's father found out I was pregnant, he also wanted nothing to do with me. To make matters worse, I was placed on a leave of absence from the restaurant. I was twenty-three years old, pregnant, and alone. I knew in my heart that I would not be able to raise my baby. I wasn't even sure how I was going to take care of myself.

Back in Detroit, where I was staying at the time, I was put in touch with the Methodist Home, which provided support to unwed mothers, including an adoption service, and I joined the Methodist church. A woman I had met at the restaurant, whom I will be forever grateful to, took me into her home, and I found a job babysitting to earn a little bit of money. When my daughter was finally born, I named her Stephanie Rose. But I never saw her, never held her. I knew it would be harder to let her go if I did. She was put into foster care for nearly three years before being adopted by a loving couple. But I didn't find that out until many years later. I thought of Stephanie every day as I slowly got back on my feet.

Fast forward thirty years. I had married, but never had any other children, although I did have three step-daughters. I was living in Ft. Lauderdale when one day I received a letter. It had been sent to my parents' home and my sister had forwarded it to me. The return address was "The Methodist Home in Detroit," and I knew right away that it had something to do with my daughter. For reasons that I can't fully explain, it took me two months to open the letter. I suppose I was simply nervous about what the letter would say. As it turned out, the letter only asked me to contact the home, which I did. I was told that my daughter was looking for me and asked if I wanted to fill out the paperwork to allow my information to be released to her, and I did. And then I waited to hear from the daughter I had given up for adoption so many years ago.

It was Thanksgiving week when I spoke to her for the first time. I had learned that she had been renamed Gail by her adoptive family and that she was married and had three sons. A conference call had been arranged so that Gail and I and both our husbands could all participate. It was with much excitement and just as much nervousness that we finally heard each other's voices. What an amazing feeling! Our husbands both said that Gail and I sounded alike and had the same vocal mannerisms and inflections. We talked for over an hour, and I began to learn about the daughter I never knew. Before we hung up we made arrangements to meet in early December. Gail would fly to Ft. Lauderdale and we would spend the weekend together. When that moment arrived not too long afterward, we connected immediately, and the years began to melt away.

With my daughter Gail

I learned that Gail's adoptive mother had died the previous year. That's when Gail, with her father's blessing, began her search for me. She was still living in Detroit, a successful financial advisor, and volunteered at the Methodist home

123

where she had once been in foster care. It was on the one year anniversary of her mother's death, just as Gail was starting to get depressed that she had not heard from me, that she received the news that I had been located, and she truly believes that her adoptive mother had a hand in our reunion. When she learned that she had been named Stephanie Rose at birth, she told me that is what she would have named a daughter if she'd had one.

Our first weekend together went quickly, but we continued to get to know each other through regular phone calls. I went to Detroit and met her family, including my three grandsons, and Gail had a big party for me while I was there. Twenty years have now passed since my daughter and I were reunited. And while I had to let her go when she was a baby, I am so proud of the beautiful person she has become and couldn't be happier to have her back in my life.

Apples

Helen Muchow

"An apple a day keeps the doctor away." For most folks this old adage is a simple reminder of the goodness of the ever-popular fruit. But when you're surrounded by apples every day, you don't need much reminding.

When my husband William and I were married in 1946, we lived with my mother on Tonawanda Creek Road in the north end of Clarence. Ironically it was the same road I had lived on in my early childhood before the family moved to a farm on nearby Goodrich Road. William had also lived on Goodrich on the farm across the street from ours, and it hadn't taken me long to develop a keen dislike for him. Almost five years older than me, William used to bring his horses across the road to our farm to water them from our well, and he teased me relentlessly whenever he saw me. He also was a good friend of my older brother, and eventually we both grew up and were in my brother's wedding. Suddenly the teasing stopped and a mutual affection took its place.

I graduated from Clarence High School in 1941 and took a job as a bookkeeper. Willie, as his friends called him, was drafted into World War II and stationed in the Pacific. We exchanged letters until he came home in 1945, and we were married a year later.

In 1950, after living with my mother for several years, Willie and I bought my cousin's farm on Tonawanda Creek Road. Originally belonging to my grandfather, the small farm had a comfortable white frame home, two big barns with chickens, pigs, and a cow, and row upon row of apple trees. As our family grew to include four children, apples were as much a part of our lives as peanut butter and jelly. The apple orchard provided us with an abundance of applesauce, apple butter, and apple pies, and we began selling apples and sweet apple cider.

Willie worked at Harrison's in Lockport, so much of the tending to the apples, the animals, the crops and the kids was my responsibility. Besides the usual housework and laundry that life with four children demands, I fed the animals, worked in the gardens, drove the tractor and, of course, cooked and baked. In time I could peel an apple in a matter of seconds, and I can't even begin to guess how many thousands of apples I peeled over the years! In addition to the apples, we always had a garden full of vegetables—beans, corn, tomatoes, squash, pumpkin, etc.—and we grew and sold hay, wheat, and oats. Willie worked hard after work and on the weekends, and our days were long and busy.

We grew several varieties of apples, including McIntosh, Cortland, and Red Delicious, on about fifty trees. Willie kept the trees trimmed, and each week he sprayed them with oil to protect them from insects and disease. As the trees died or were damaged, they were replaced with new ones. We sold about five hundred bushels of apples a year, and during the autumn apple season we sold about fifty gallons of sweet cider a week. It took ten bushels of apples to make one fifty gallon barrel of cider, and only the best apples were used—never any that had fallen to the ground. The apples were taken to a cider mill in Niagara County to be pressed and then we sold the cider from our home. It was always such good cider that people would drive from miles around to buy it. When we had any surplus apples, they were given away to friends or donated to the Salvation Army. As the kids got older they all helped on the farm, and picking apples was a family affair. Friends and relatives often came to pick and sort the apples too, and I'd make lunch for everyone who came to help

No one ever had to wonder what I would bring to the potluck dinners at church—eight apple pies was my standard contribution. But mishaps did happen. One day, after making the church pies and setting them on a card table to cool in the living room, my two oldest girls, Karen and Carol, who were about six and seven at the time, decided to play chase. One scooted under the card table then tried to stand up, and my morning's work went flying to the floor. There were none of my apple pies at the church supper that night!

Another mishap occurred one day that made an even bigger mess. Willie always made one barrel of hard cider each year, which was kept in the cellar. I happened to be downstairs and noticed strange sounds and bubbles coming from the barrel. Fortunately Willie was home that day, and I called him to come down. Now, as hard cider ferments, it gives off gases, which are allowed to escape through a small hole at the top of the barrel. Once the process is complete, the hole is sealed with a bung, or a cork. Well, as Willie came down the stairs and saw what was happening to the barrel, he realized the bung had been put in too soon and that pressure was building inside the barrel. To avert a bigger disaster, he grabbed a baseball bat and smashed the bung on the barrel, and apple cider shot out like a fountain. Now, I also canned my apple products and our vegetables and had about two hundred jars on nearby shelves, which were now totally covered in cider. What a mess! It took me hours to clean everything up, and you can be sure we never again put the bung in the barrel too soon.

Our children grew up and started their own lives, and my youngest daughter Lynn eventually bought a house down the road from ours. In time I had eight grandchildren—and then eight great-grandchildren. Ironically our only son, Donald, who had not been overly fond of our apple orchard when he was a youngster, bought his own apple orchard in Michigan.

We sold our apples for over fifty years, until Willie died in 2006. I lived on the farm for another eight years, but at ninety years old, after having spent my whole life living only on Tonawanda Creek Road and Goodrich Road, it was time to move on. The farm and apple orchard were sold to a neighboring farmer, and I now live at Brompton Heights, a beautiful facility in Williamsville. But on my wall, along with pictures of my family, are pictures of—as you might guess—apples, the perfect reminder of my busy but happy life.

The farm and apple orchard on Tonawanda Creek Road in Clarence

A portion of the proceeds from *Reflections* will be donated to Clarence Senior Citizens, Inc., a 501(c)(3) not-for-profit organization that administers the Clarence Senior Center. Learn more at clarenceseniorcenter.org.

Made in the USA
Middletown, DE
27 June 2015